T0129370

From THERE *to* HERE

A Journey from the Grip of Communism to America's Freedoms and Opportunities

HERMAN HAENERT

ARCHWAY
PUBLISHING

Archway Publishing books may be ordered through booksellers or by contacting:

Archway Publishing
1663 Liberty Drive
Bloomington, IN 47403
www.archwaypublishing.com
1 (888) 242-5904

ISBN: 978-1-4808-7481-7 (sc)
ISBN: 978-1-4808-7482-4 (e)

Library of Congress Control Number: 2019901570

Print information available on the last page.

Archway Publishing rev. date: 03/14/2019

CONTENTS

FOREWORD

I would like to dedicate this book to my parents, Erich and Tosca Haenert, who gave up everything they owned to be free - and most of all, for a better opportunity for their three sons. Thank you, Pa and Ma, for your broken English that told the real story to so many who would listen – and who would welcome you to the small American community of Scales Mound, Illinois.

To my beautiful wife, Judy, who has endured Herman's many entrepreneurial challenges with open arms - a tough assignment. I love you.

Additionally, I dedicate this book to our children, Jay and Heidi, and our grandchildren: Zach, Dillon and Benjamin. This is a historical Haenert family documentary.

To America: One Nation under God, Indivisible, with Liberty, Opportunity and Justice for All.

Herman Haenert, **Author**

About the Writer/Editor: https://kelliebgormly.com

INTRODUCTION

November 9, 2018

As I write this, I think about what happened 29 years ago today – when Americans turned on the television and watched with awe what was happening across the Atlantic Ocean: Germans were dismantling the dreadful Berlin Wall, which had separated Germany since 1961. Block by block, chip by chip, the wall that imprisoned East Germans and separated families came down.

And, 80 ago on Nov. 9 and 10, Kristallnacht – the vicious Nazi attack against Jewish businesses, synagogues and other buildings, which had their windows smashed - happened in Nazi Germany.

This book is the story of Herman Haenert, an American citizen who spent his younger years in Germany, under both Nazi and Communist rule. He lived through these nightmares – then, crossed an ocean to build a successful life in the United States, a free country.

Herman's life story combines inspiration with a history lesson. I hope you enjoy reading it as much as we have enjoyed telling it.

Kellie Gormly, Writer and Editor

Chapter 1

Haenert Roots

Herman Otto Haenert

Born: June 7, 1939 in Ramin, Germany. This is about 139 kilometers – or 86.15 miles, in American terms - northeast of Berlin, now near the Polish border.

Herman is the youngest of three boys. The oldest brother, Carl, was born in 1926; Horst followed in 1934.

Both of his parents were raised on farms, which is what most people did back in those days, Herman says. And he, himself, grew up on a farm – a family tradition that goes back decades.

Father: Erich Paul Hänert

Erich Paul Hänert – the original German spelling, later replaced in America by Haenert without the umlaut – was born on March 31, 1897 in Kahlwinkel, a tiny town in the state of Saxony-Anhalt near Naumburg. Erich was one of eight children born to Leopold and Matilda (Haumann) Haenert. His brothers and sisters were: Karl, Kurt, Ellie, Lisbeth, Konrad, Tosca, and Oswald.

Erich's family owned a farm that still stands today, though an heir - Karl Haenert, the last of the Haenerts to own the homeplace - sold the property in the 1990s. During the Russian occupation, the lack of building materials prevented the maintenance of buildings on the farm. Consequently, everything was left a mess, requiring a lot of money to repair after the wall came down. The family did not have the money and consequently had to sell at a large discount.

Erich grew up on the farm and had that professional background, but Erich also at one point studied accounting. He also knew a great deal about fertilizer, a topic that came in handy for farmers and eventually played a role in Erich's pathway to America.

Herman remembers his father as a deep thinker who was very entrepreneurial and resourceful. Erich served in the German Army in World War I, with the Russia-based cavalry; he, like the rest of the family, was quite a horse lover, both in and out of the military. The family bred and raised horses for the German Cavalry; this was a big part of their farming income. When he returned home after what was then called The Great War, Erich decided that he wanted to immigrate to the United States. He went to America in 1923, but later returned to his home country in 1933.

Erich was a typical German father of the era, in that he wasn't particularly close emotionally to his children; that is what Mom provided. Dad's focus was on work and income, but he had a fun side and a good sense of humor.

"He was very much occupied with many facets of life and making a living, and making a better living," Herman says. "When he said something, it was meaningful. He was a better listener than me. He was a very bright man."

Herman had little contact with his father's parents. He never met his grandfather, as he had died in 1930. Family records recovered after the Russian occupation indicate that Grandpa Leopold was on his death bed and called in a notary public to execute his will. Herman has found a copy of the will, which for 1930 was very detailed and professionally executed. Herman's father's share of the estate was 3,000 Reichsmark (approximately $13,000 in U.S. dollars in 1930), plus 12 acres of land. However, there was one stipulation: Erich could only claim his share if he was living in Germany. Herman only met his grandmother once, in 1945, as she lived 246 miles from Ramin. This was not an unusual family situation in an era when the only civilian mode of transportation was a horse-drawn wagon, bicycle or train.

In 1980, Erich passed away while Herman and his wife, Judy, were on their way to Germany for a vacation including the passion play in Oberammergau. This was a tour organized by the couple's church, St. Mark Lutheran in Rockford, Illinois, and their friend, Pastor Viereck. They were ready to board the plane at Chicago's O'Hare airport to Germany when they got the terrible news about Erich's passing; their daughter, Heidi, had notified the airline. Thanks to this just-in-time news, Herman and Judy could change their plans and be there for the funeral etc. Following the funeral, Herman and Judy continued their trip to Germany, meeting the group on the Rhine River cruise to continue the tour.

Mother: Tosca Marie Kunze

Toska (pronounced "Toshka") was born on August 26, 1899 in Mertendorf, a small community in Saxony-Anhalt. Her parents are Oswin and Emilie Kunze. Toska (the spelling later changed to "Tosca") was one of four children: two sisters who died of a very young age, and a brother, Walter, who farmed the original homestead until his death. Herman never met his grandfather - Oswin, who preferred to spend his time hunting, fishing and socializing in the pub, rather than working. Emilie – who was born in Eisleben, Martin Luther's hometown, and grew up in Bernsdorf – was a very loving grandmother. The monastery Schulpforte – a wealthy and influential monastery in Naumburg that closed during the Reformation - had files on the Kunze family dating back to 1345. Herman has some relatives who live near Naumburg today. The monastery's original buildings still stand, but since have expanded and been modernized, and turned into a school.

Like her future husband, Tosca also was raised on a farm, located in nearby Mertendorf. They met as Erich visited the Kunze farm to sell them horses. That farm is still in the Kunze family, to this day. Young Herman also knew his maternal grandmother, but not his grandfather, who had passed away.

The Kunze homestead is still in the family dating back to 1750. Armin Kunze, Herman's second cousin, and two of Armin's children live in the original and expanded buildings. Some of the old buildings have been torn down and modernized; one became a four-room bed and breakfast. The family is still in the horse business, and they have an indoor riding facility complete with riding lessons.

Tosca may have spent most of her young life working on the farm, but at one point she went to school to learn how to cook – not to be a professional chef, but just to cook really well for her family. And Mom, with a passion for food, did just that, Herman recalls.

"She guarded her cookbooks with everything," he says. You can read the remarkable story of how Tosca guarded her beloved cookbooks during the Russian invasion in the next chapter.

Mother Tosca was a very outgoing and determined person, Herman recalls.

"She's the type of person who would never take no for answer," he says. "She was very driven."

Mom may have been strict with discipline, but overall, she was a loving woman and the "best wife and mom," Herman says.

Tosca passed away in 1985.

Erich and Tosca Come to America

Long before Herman immigrated to America, his parents crossed the Atlantic for their own adventure in American farming.

When Erich returned from World War I to Kahlwinkel, the economy was very weak. People were fiercely competing for limited jobs in a country impoverished after the war that ended in 1918, so the offer from the Lutheran Church in Germany was tempting. The church partnered with the Lutheran Church in the United States to send its German members out to America, a country with a growing population, to work jobs in certain industries like farming.

Erich's talents in working the land and his knowledge about fertilizer led him overseas to a farming job in the tiny town of Scales Mound, Ilinois - the heart of the American Midwest and a settlement of a lot of German families. The Lutheran Church sponsored Erich and many other immigrants, who would come to America for new jobs with sponsoring families. In Illinois, the Hesselbacher family hosted Erich on their farm and put him to work, performing tasks like taking care of animals, and plowing the fields.

"They did everything to earn a living in those days," Herman says. "They raised the crops, milked cows … you name it."

At that time, the United States was in an immigration boom: Between 1900 and 1920, the country admitted more than 14.5 million immigrants. World War I greatly reduced immigration from Europe, but mass immigration resumed after the war.

Erich was one of the millions of Europeans who left their homelands to come to America, the land of opportunity. He boarded a ship – the Mount Clay, built in 1904 - in Hamburg, and arrived about 10 days later at New York's Ellis Island on November 12, 1923, with some 1,200 fellow passengers seeking a new life.

"He was wanting to better himself financially," Herman says. "He had an entrepreneurial mind and a progressive spirit."

When Erich left Germany in 1923, he already had met his future wife, Tosca. He had met Tosca through his family's business of raising horses for the German Cavalry, and selling the animals to other people around Germany – including Tosca's family. The two young adults felt a connection and kept in touch when Erich went to America.

Then, two years after he arrived, the Hesselbacher family agreed to sponsor Tosca, too, and bring her over to Illinois. She departed on August 22, 1925, from Bremen on a ship called Columbus. On September 4, 1925 - a week after Tosca arrived in America - she and Erich went to Dubuque, Iowa, and got married there. A new family was born.

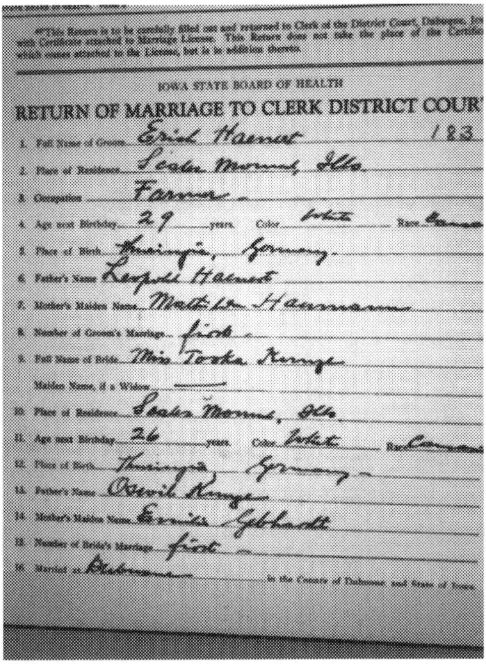

This Return is to be carefully filled out and returned to Clerk of the District Court, Dubuque, Io[wa] with Certificate attached to Marriage License. This Return does not take the place of the Certific[ate] which comes attached to the License, but is in addition thereto.

IOWA STATE BOARD OF HEALTH

RETURN OF MARRIAGE TO CLERK DISTRICT COUR[T]

1. Full Name of Groom Erich Haenert 183
2. Place of Residence Scales Mound, Ills.
3. Occupation Farmer
4. Age next Birthday 29 years. Color White Race
5. Place of Birth Thuringia, Germany
6. Father's Name Leopold Haenert
7. Mother's Maiden Name Mathilde Haemann
8. Number of Groom's Marriage first
9. Full Name of Bride Miss Toska Kunze

Maiden Name, if a Widow —

10. Place of Residence Scales Mound, Ills.
11. Age next Birthday 26 years. Color White Race
12. Place of Birth Thuringia, Germany
13. Father's Name Oswil Kunze
14. Mother's Maiden Name Ernestine Gebhardt
15. Number of Bride's Marriage first
16. Married at Dubuque in the County of Dubuque, and State of Iowa

Erich Haenert /Tosca Kunze Marriage License

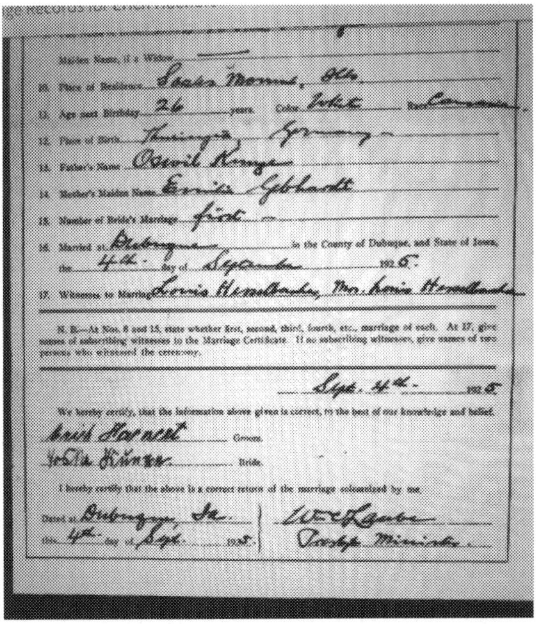

Maiden Name, if a Widow —

10. Place of Residence Scales Mound, Ills.
11. Age next Birthday 26 years. Color White Race
12. Place of Birth Thuringia, Germany
13. Father's Name Oswil Kunze
14. Mother's Maiden Name Ernestine Gebhardt
15. Number of Bride's Marriage first
16. Married at Dubuque in the County of Dubuque, and State of Iowa, the 4th day of September 1926.
17. Witnesses to Marriage Louis Hembacher, Mrs. Louis Hembacher

N. B.—At Nos. 8 and 15, state whether first, second, third, fourth, etc., marriage of each. At 17, give names of subscribing witnesses to the Marriage Certificate. If no subscribing witnesses, give names of two persons who witnessed the ceremony.

Sept. 4th 1926

We hereby certify, that the information above given is correct, to the best of our knowledge and belief.

Erich Haenert Groom.

Tosca Kunze Bride.

I hereby certify that the above is a correct return of the marriage solemnized by me.

Dated at Dubuque, Ia. this 4th day of Sept. 1926.

Presby. Minister.

A year after the couple married, they left Illinois to move to Mauston, Wisconsin. There, they lived with Tosca's uncle on his farm. Erich and Tosca ran the Gebhardt family farm, doing all of the farm duties from 1926 to 1932. During their time in Wisconsin, the couple's first child, Karl, was born.

Erich's father, Leopold, included a stipulation in his will that Erich could only claim his share of the inheritance – money and a portion of the farm - if he were living in Germany. Leopold died in 1930, and in 1932, Erich and Tosca returned to Germany to collect his inheritance and start a new life in their ancestral home.

Herman's grandfather's directive said, "I will put money into a savings account, and it will draw interest until you come home. It was very explicitly detailed ... I was very impressed."

Erich and Tosca drove their car from Wisconsin to the New York shore, where they sold the car at the dock. Tosca brought along her kitchen stove and actually took it onto the ship with her to bring home; Herman remembers this stove, a "big old clunker." Once they arrived back in Germany, they returned to Kahlwinkel, where Herman's grandmother was still living; she died in 1949. Leopold's directives in his will seemed to ensure that his eight kids, Erich included, would take care of his wife – and they did.

The inheritance was divided among the eight siblings, and Erich's share included two horses, a wagon, chickens, two hogs, and two cows. Then, Erich's youngest brother, Oswald, helped the family make the trip from Kahlwinkel, and then begin a new life and new settlement in the rural area in Ramin.

According to the Ramin Chronical published in 2000, Otto von Ramin founded Ramin in 1267. At the time, royalty – identified by "von" in a name - ruled Germany, which had a lot of smaller states that became kingdoms under Napoleon.

Modern Ramin has a governing Burgermeister – the German word for mayor – and an older population of mostly retired people. The town's pride is the Feldsteinkirche (Fieldstone Church), which was built in the 13th century and is still a place of worship today. The church, which is on the historical registry, still uses a communion chalice and bread plate from the Martin Luther era. The cobblestone main street, called Dorfstrasse, began as a horse-and-buggy road, and now hosts automobiles. It is hard to imagine that buildings and roads constructed centuries ago are still standing!

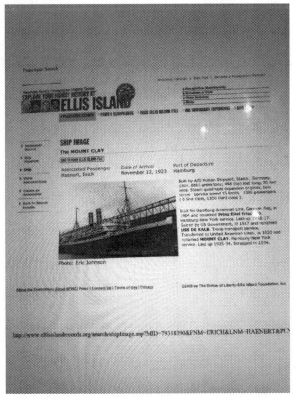

Erich Haenert's Ship "Mount Clay"

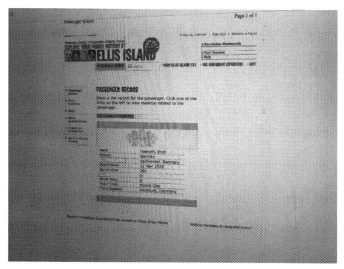

Erich Haenert Passenger Record

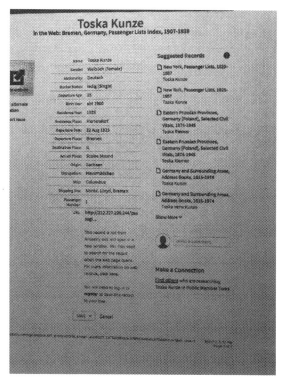

Toska Kunze Passenger List

The ship (Columbus) Toska Kunze Haenert's
passage to America in 1925

Life on the Depression-era German Farm

At the time, during the early 1930s, Germany – and especially certain industries, like agriculture – suffered from the Great Depression. The economic disaster that began with the American stock market crash in 1929 didn't just affect the United States; the Great Depression hit areas, including Europe, around the world.

German farmers who owned huge chunks of land suffered financially when prices of their key crop, sugar beets, fell sharply due to too much supply and limited demand. Many of the big farms went bankrupt. A group of wealthy people from Berlin got together and purchased the land holdings. The investors subdivided the farmland into 68 parcels near Ramin – the land became a new settlement on SchmagerowerWeg, with 17 houses and farmsteads - and the Haenerts bought one of the 17 homesteads to start a new family farm.

The Haenert farm – about 60 acres, divided into three parcels - raised chickens and geese, and grew crops including potatoes, rye, wheat and sugar beets. Horses and humans did the plowing on the farm, which had two main buildings: One housed grain, and the other housed straw and hay for the animals. Barn cats controlled the rodent population.

Farmers did everything by hand back in those days: planting the crops, caring for them, and pulling weeds in an era before commercial weed control.

"Of course, it was very, very labor-intensive," Herman says. "It was a labor of love just to survive in those days."

While running his farm, Erich also started a bank for the farmers, and many of them deposited their money. In this pre-electronic banking era, Erich stored much of his bank's money as physical cash in a giant safe at home – a safe that was destroyed during the Russian invasion, covered in a later chapter. Erich also played a leading role in establishing a volunteer fire department in 1935 in Ramin.

It wasn't just the farm workers who toiled for the goods the family would sell; Tosca tended her own huge, prolific vegetable and flower garden, just for her family. The garden grew "everything you can think about," Herman says: cabbage, lettuce, tomatoes, berry bushes, cherry trees, white asparagus, and lots of flowers. This garden met many food needs before grocery stores existed. Tosca always baked her own bread, too.

Speaking of cooking and baking, Herman recalls a frequent meal schedule among Germans at the time, and even today. People typically would eat two breakfasts – one around 7 a.m., and one around 10 a.m. - then, eat lunch at noon, have coffee and cake at 3 p.m., and eat the evening meal around 6 p.m.

With no electricity, the German kitchen of the early 20th century is difficult to imagine for modern cooks: People had no refrigerators, no electric ovens, and even no ice. Everything that needed cooling was in the basement, and meat was preserved in brine to keep it from spoiling. Families and farmers would harvest crops like crazy and stock up for the winter, and they did a lot of canning – not as a fun hobby like people do today, but a matter of eating and survival.

"You worked all summer to survive the winter," Herman says. "Those farmers way back then were very, very tough people."

When the Haenerts returned to Germany, they already had their first son, Karl. Then, in 1934, Horst was born – and five years later, Herman joined the family.

Following is the detailed family tree.

The Erich Haenert Descendants

The brothers are Carl Haenert, Horst Haenert, Herman Haenert

Herman and Judy have two children: Hans and Heidi.

Hans is married to Dawn. They have one son, Zachary.

Zachary is married to Jenny. They have no children.

Heidi is married to David Dinter. They have two children: Dillon and Benjamin, neither of whom are married.

Carl is deceased. He was married to Jean, and they have three daughters: Linda, Karla and Paula.

Linda is married to Cal Schafer. They have three daughters: Meghan, Abby and Olivia.

Meghan is married to Matt Randecker. They have two children: Wyatt and Cora.

Abby is married to Jerry Meade. They have two children: Harlow and Cash.

Horst is deceased. He was married to Harriett, who is also deceased. They have two children: Susan and Sarah.

Susan is married to Bill Ertmer. They have three children: Ryan, Allison and Jesse.

Allison is married to Charlie Twombly. They have two children: Avery and Amy.

Sarah is married to Andrew Kingsbury. They have four children: Melissa, Mathew, Misti and Michael.

The family tree includes relatives living in Germany, and Herman still has contact with them.

Karola and Dieter Krause live in Laucha, Germany. Karola is the daughter of Karl Haenert, Herman's first cousin and son of Konrad Harnert.

Armin Kunze lives in Mertendorf, Germany. He is the son of Walter Kunze, Herman's first cousin from his mother's side.

Chapter 2

Early Childhood during WWII Germany

People born in the past few decades cannot imagine the childhood of a kid born in the 1930s in Germany – an often-joyless youth where the trauma of war colored everything. As was the case with many families, World War II took both Herman's father, Erich, and oldest brother – Carl, then only 16 - away from home because they were drafted into the German Army. This creates a major void in a boy's life.

And then, there is the constant fear of getting killed, even among the youngest civilians.

"The first things I remember are things that happened during the war," Herman says about his life. "My early memories are about the war and the planes coming and bombing all around us."

Herman's family dug out a bunker below the Ramin-based farm. Herman recalls huddling with family members in the crude, dirty hole in the ground as the bombing planes would fly overhead at night. The planes bombed rural German areas as well as cities, so people like

Herman's family faced the same danger living on farms as did residents of cities like Berlin.

Because Ramin was located near Stettin – now a Polish city called Szczecin - the city was a major railroad hub and a major center of the German weapons industry, and the home of the German automaker Stoewer. Allied air raids in 1944 destroyed some 65 percent of Stettin's buildings, and wiped out almost all of the city center, industry and the seaport on the Oder River. During the destruction of Stettin, nearly 400,000 Germans fled or were expelled from the city; on April 26, 1945, the Soviet Red Army captured Stettin. After the war, although the Potsdam Agreement did not specify this, Poland acquired Stettin and its population, which was greatly reduced for a few decades.

Sights and Sounds

Herman remembers very well the sounds of the B-24s and B-25s, mostly British planes, that severely damaged the land around the Haenert homestead. He can't forget how war literally destroys innocent people's lives, and civilians did their best to warn each other.

Young Herman, just 5 or so, remembers his father riding his bicycle around the neighborhood and warning people that the bombers were coming. Each neighbor had erected a pole with a piece of metal plowshares attached. My father would use a hammer and bang on the plowshares - a crude farming tool used as a civil-defense device - to warn everyone about the possibility of a bombing attack. Then, everyone fled to individual family bunkers.

"I remember running into the bunker and hearing the planes coming," Herman says. "It is very, very vivid waiting for the bombs to drop."

After the planes finished their bombing missions, carnage remained. The site and stench of dead bodies strewn throughout the fields will be forever embedded in Herman's mind. As an inquisitive young boy, he walked across the fields to view the large holes left by the explosive bombs.

This war-torn environment left few opportunities for childhood games and fun, but little children in the neighborhood sometimes entertained themselves by playing Fussball together. The playtime never lasted long, as World War II was raging – and, the worst was yet to come for Germans in 1945. In that final year of the war, the Soviet Union's Red Army invaded Germany for total destruction of everything in its path.

Fleeing the Red Army

Herman's family and all other residents in the farming community had to evacuate their town – an experience depicted in the German movie "Die Flucht" – and escape before the Russians arrived, if they wanted to live. They loaded everyone onto a horse-drawn wagon, with limited food and water, and headed west - away from the Russians attacking from the east.

The slow-moving caravan was a demanding challenge of survival. As food supplies dwindled, the staple became wild rabbits that people killed by throwing accurate and lucky rocks, instead of bullets. People killed pigeons with stone-loaded slingshots. And nobody, no matter how thirsty, could drink water – hauled from the brooks – until it had been boiled.

"It was our entire community. We all, like an old wagon train, headed west to meet the American Army and get away from the Russians," Herman recalls. "I remember that like it was yesterday. When the Russians came in, it was a total nightmare."

The family didn't make it all the way to the safety of the Americans; Russian troops intercepted the Haenerts on the trail, so the family made plans to turn back toward their hometown. It was very difficult to regroup, since the Russians stole a lot of the horses in the caravan;

Red Army members rode off on bareback, laughing and drinking vodka. They ransacked the wagons, knowing that most people brought their most cherished possessions.

The neighbors managed to regroup, shared remaining horses and found free-roaming oxen in a pasture; the people hooked the oxen to the wagons to start the trek toward Ramin. Finding feed for the hungry animals was very difficult.

At the last stop before reaching the home destination, a number of people in the caravan, including Herman's father, acted as scouts to see what was left of Ramin, which had become a ghost town. They found their home destroyed, pillaged and burned to ashes.

"Everybody turned to go back to the town and try to get back home with the remaining horses and wagon," Herman says. "We then found out that our place was completely burned to the ground, so there was nothing there."

Herman's father was a banker for the farming community along with being a farmer; his office was in the farm house, along with a large safe. Although the safe had been left open, the Russians could not figure out its thick doors and blew them open, thinking the money was inside the doors. That action started a fire that destroyed the entire farm buildings and living quarters. And then, there was the Russian pillaging.

"They come, and they try to confiscate everything they can," Herman recalls about the Russian troops, who seemed envious of possessions like watches and took them. Communist Red Army members apparently didn't have a lot of items common to Germans, including modern conveniences like flushing toilets. They had never ridden a bicycle, and Herman can still see them falling on their stupid behinds.

"They were basically looking for things that they can steal - whatever they can steal from you," he explains.

The Russians may have burned and stolen the Haenerts' property, but Herman's mother managed to outsmart them by planning ahead and burying family treasures in the barn before fleeing. Tosca buried cherished items like some old family dishes, cookbooks and photos, and these heirlooms survived the Russian invasion in the dirt. She buried them in different places throughout the barn under the hay and straw.

Yet, sadly, all other family possessions were totally destroyed. All the family members had left were their possessions in the wagon, one horse, and one cow. How do you start over from basically nothing and a broken political system?

Herman's parents surely were strong people, driven by finding ways of survival for themselves and the family. Watching neighbors helping neighbors, pooling resources, and leaning on each other's shoulders was an incredible experience for Herman that has stayed with him for life. The exposure to desperation, fear of dying, caring and sharing with your neighbors and those in need formed the foundation for Herman's drive for success – and, to make a better life for his family.

It wasn't just property that the Red Army destroyed and stole, and it wasn't just the Nazis in concentration camps committing atrocities. Members of the brutal Russian Army raped countless civilian German women, which is a recorded historical fact though something people try to forget.

More than two million German women were raped by soldiers of the Red Army. It was a feature of Russia's liberation and occupation of eastern Germany at the end of World War II that is familiar enough to historians, but Russia does not acknowledge it enough. It is written that for many German women, the memory was something they sublimated and never spoke about to their husbands returning from the front. Sadly, many rape victims had abortions or were treated for the syphilis they caught. Of the children born out of rape, many were abandoned.

Although other women in the community did not fare that well, Herman's mother was spared this crime – though a Russian soldier did try. Thank God he didn't succeed. The loud screams of the group, and possible retaliation with an ax and shovel, scared him away. Sadly, one of Herman's relatives was a rape victim; a Russian soldier forcefully accosted her, and she gave birth to a child.

A Train Trip to Remember

Having come back home to Ramin and finding everything was gone, the Haenerts initially spent a few months in 1945 with some nearby family – a niece of his mother's - in an intact house.

The Russian soldiers continued to harass every household, knocking on doors at all hours of the night looking for people who had been identified as possible opposition leaders to the Russians. Herman remembers the knocks on the door and being terribly afraid. Every day, the news spread that numerous innocent neighbors were hauled away, confined and interrogated – and Herman's father was one of those people. Erich had been identified as one of leaders of the community; the Russians had to make sure by intimidation that everyone would follow the Russian rules of occupation. Panic, violence and the execution of innocent people are recorded in the Ramin Chronicle. Raids and rape were still the agenda of the Red Army.

During that time, it was survival of the fittest. Typhoid fever, introduced by bad food and infected wells, was killing a lot of the inhabitants. Acquiring food and water was a daily chore for family survival, and the majority of the farmers had lost most of the livestock.

According to the Ramin Chronicle, only 11 horses and 20 cattle, including four cows, remained upon the return to Ramin from the evacuation in 1945. Ramin also became a place for refugees from other Eastern countries. The population in Ramin in 1939 was 593; because of refugees, the population increased to 720 in early 1946.

The Haenerts survived on water, potatoes stored from the previous harvest, gravy made from hand-ground wheat flour, in-season fruit, and pigeons and sparrows shot with a slingshot. During this time of scarcity, a black market for food developed.

The struggle to survive at the farm became insurmountable, so as the next transitional stop, Herman's parents decided to return to his father's and mother's hometown of Kahlwinkel and Mertendorf to regroup and lay out a plan for survival and the future of Herman's family. Since most of the earthly belongings were lost during the fire the Red Army set, going home to Kahlwinkel and Mertendorf was critical for survival. Neither Kahlwinkel nor Mertendorf was subject to Allied bombings, and the agriculture/ livestock industry was not drastically impacted by the war. There was food for survival, and the outreach and warmth of extended family members to help Herman's family made the difficult journey a key for renewal.

Kahlwinkel was only accessible by train, via Berlin. The family boarded a train in Grambow, the nearest train station to Ramin, to connect with a train in Berlin to Kahlwinkel. When we arrived in Berlin, the city had been left a wasteland with vast piles of rubble everywhere. Other areas were rows of building walls with collapsed interiors - the skeletons of a destroyed city. Palaces, museums, churches, monuments, cultural sites, and the living quarters of millions fell victim to the bombs. Some 50,000 people died, and some 600,000 apartments were destroyed; thousands of Germans were homeless and living in the rubble.

The sites and smell of the city in 1945 are still very vivid in Herman's mind.

Herman's Uncle Willie - along with his wife, Agnes, and daughter, Troudchen - lived in Berlin and survived the horrible experience. Uncle Willie is the key person later mentioned in the escape from Communist East Germany.

With the help of Uncle Willie, who came on his bicycle to meet the family, getting onto a train wasn't that simple: With all of the evacuating and moving – and war-torn areas where railroads were destroyed – what trains did run were completely stuffed to capacity. The only way to get on a train ride was to sit on the roof – yes, the roof, in the open air. And that is what Erich, Toska and their boys, Herman and Horst, did, with only the clothes they were wearing. Thankfully, roof passengers didn't slide off, but the journey was frightening. The trip was six-plus hours, with no bathroom stops. Uncle Willie brought the family rye bread and sausage for the journey.

"You had to lie down when you got to the underpasses," Herman remembers. "That was quite a memorable and impressionable trip for a kid who is only 6 years old."

The family arrived in Kahlwinkel safely, and Herman started school in the first grade. They lived in Herman's father's home place, along with his brother, Konrad, and his family. Herman made friends and remembers Helmut Dietrich, whose parents owned the bar in Kahlwinkel. Herman recalls the specialty served in the bar: beer soup, which is really good stuff for a 6-year-old. Other food was not so tasty: While in Kahlwinkel, Herman's grandmother served lamb "mutton," made with meat from adult sheep. It was so bad, and to this day, Herman has not eaten any "lamb meat."

Throughout the time in Kahlwinkel, Herman and his family visited many of the relatives living in the surrounding area, accessible by horse and buggy. They celebrated special occasions and holidays together.

During those eight months in Kahlwinkel, the family initiated plans to start over again Ramin. The farm land was still there and, with the help of family, they decided to return to the ruins of their farm and rebuild. Herman's Uncle Konrad loaned the family a wagon, two horses and other necessities, and they made the trip – this time, without Russian interference - back to Ramin.

The trek from Kahlwinkel with horse and wagon to Ramin - about 250 miles - had many experiences along the way. Herman recalls many instances of finding places to bed down for the evening, and the fear of people trying to interfere. The angst and the memories of the terrible war were deeply embedded in the minds of the people met along the journey back to Ramin. It also brought back memories of the wagon trip trying to escape from the Red Army.

Side Story: Carl F. Haenert, the Soldier

In the summer of 1943, before he'd reached his 17th birthday, Carl was drafted into the German Army. Her served until 1945 as an infantryman and reached the rank of Sergeant. After he underwent basic training and indoctrination, Carl went to Italy in September to face combat against the Allied forces. Carl's army, facing high casualties, was gradually retreating north when his squad of 15 men took a forward-observation position. As the Germans were setting up their equipment, Allied forces – less than 100 yards away – opened fire. Both the man to Carl's right and left died before his machine gun was ready.

An Allied bullet tore a gash into Carl's left hip, but a metal cigarette case he carried in his jacket's lower-left pocket prevented major damage to his internal organs; Carl slowed the bleeding with a tourniquet. With his counter-fire, Carl was the only man in his unit able to escape; he was taken to a German field hospital and convalesced through the early winter of 1944.

Now, as a lance corporal, Carl returned to battle on the Eastern front, where the Red Army was invading; he became a part of forces in what was then Czechoslovakia. Weary members of the German Army, as Carl later shared, began to realize that their cause was lost by early 1945, and defeat was inevitable. The Red Army captured what was left of the German forces, which had shrunk dramatically due to casualties and desertions.

Carl and thousands of German comrades became the Red Army's prisoners of war, who marched for many days before reaching the place where they would be imprisoned. Carl could not trust anyone – not even his fellow Germans. They knew they were defeated and at the mercy of their brutal captors, so self-preservation became their sole goal.

During the march to the Czechoslovakian prison camp, Carl picked up a little tin on the side of the road. It was an old German mess kit filled with sugar; Carl hid it in his shirt and supplemented his rye bread and watery soup rations with the energizing sugar.

Once they arrived at the camp, the Germans discovered that this "prison" had no walls: The captives simply were confined to open fields surrounded by Russian soldiers, who would strafe the fields 2 to 3 feet above the ground where the soldiers slept to prevent escape. American-style peanut butter was a key food the Russians fed to prisoners – and, for the rest of his life, Carl could not stand to eat peanut butter.

Carl spent the summer of 1945 in POW hell, and the Russians had no clear plan on what to do about the prisoners. Then, knowing his odds of surviving into the winter were slim, Carl decided to try to escape in September. He managed to slip through the perimeter of the prison grounds and flee east into the mountains. During a risky escape trek that lasted four to five days, Carl survived by eating berries and other plant food he found. By the time Carl crossed the American lines, he was debilitated. The American Army placed Carl into its own POW barracks, but they treated the prisoners much more humanely than the Russians did.

Carl said that he and his fellow German soldiers were hoping the Americans could see the Russians' duplicity, and they were disappointed that President Harry Truman agreed to the post-war Soviet takeover of Germany that led to the Cold War.

While the American Army's S-2 intelligence branch processed Carl and the other POWs, a captain doing his paperwork noticed that Carl actually was an American citizen, born in the Midwest. The captain tried to persuade Carl to join the American Army, but Carl couldn't go through with it. Carl hadn't spoken English for 15 years and didn't think he would fit in – and, after two years in battlefields, he felt terribly homesick for his family. Meanwhile, other prisoners became suspicious of Carl with his frequent visits to the S-2 office.

Eventually, Carl left the prison and passed through the American Consulate as a free German citizen in a friend's home. But, his family remained in Russian-controlled East Germany. After observing the patterns of the guards along the border between East and West Germany, Carl tried to cross over undetected, but a Russian guard detained him. Carl convinced the interrogators that he was on his way home – then, after two years, he was reunited with his family.

After five years with his family under miserable Russian rule, Carl decided to go back to America, though he first had to sneak by the Soviet leaders in Berlin. He packed a suitcase with just a change of clothes, bought a train ticket from Grambow to Kahlwinkel, and then slipped over to the West Side at a train stop in Berlin.

We pick up Carl's and his family's story of escaping to America in chapter three. But this is how Carl's story ended: He married Jean, daughter of Louis Hesselbacher, in 1953, and the couple settled down in Scales Mound, Illinois – the same place where his parents had lived many years ago.

Carl got drafted for military service again – this time, by the American Army, in 1954. He spent eight weeks in basic training in Arkansas and Missouri. Then, the Army stationed him in Germany, where Carl served as an interpreter and driver on the west side of the country and rose to the rank of sergeant. He never approached West Berlin and the occupied zone; Carl thought the Russian leaders would capture him and take him back to East Germany if they knew he was there.

After two years in the American Army, Carl finally retired from military life for good and returned to Illinois, where he dedicated himself to farming.

Chapter 3

From Nazism to Communism

Germany surrendered to the Allies on May 5, 1945, ending the European portion of World War II; however, the war in the Pacific theater raged on until Japan's surrender on August 15.

Active combat had ended, but Germany lay in ruins and faced devastating losses in human life. Germany lost an estimated 5,533,000 military men; when added to civilian deaths, some 6.6 to 8.8 million Germans died in the terrible war.

The Haenerts, like many German families, didn't know the status of their sons who left home to fight the war – even months after it ended.

"We had no idea if he was dead or alive," Herman says about Carl, who survived.

"Multiply ourselves by tens of thousands of families; they were all separated from people who were serving," he says. "You couldn't pick up your cell phone and call anybody. A lot of families didn't find each other until a year later because they didn't know where to look."

The Soviet Takeover

Germans were soon to face a whole new nightmare after the Hitler era of the 1930s and World War II: The Soviets took over the Eastern part of the country in 1949, leading to more than four decades of Communist rule.

At the Yalta conference in February of 1945, U.S. President Franklin D. Roosevelt, British Prime Minister Winston Churchill, and Soviet Premier Joseph Stalin met to demand Germany's unconditional surrender and to plan for a post-war world. The leaders broke Germany into four occupied zones, and the Soviets ran a portion of it. This Russian occupation of Germany and Eastern Europe degenerated into the Cold War.

Later, in July and August of 1945, the "Big Three" – including new U.S. President Harry S. Truman, who replaced Roosevelt after he died in office – met near Berlin to establish conditions for Germany's war reparations. They created a Council of Foreign Ministers and an Allied Control Council, which would manage Germany's zones, the economy, and the trials for Nazi war criminals.

After the war ended, Great Britain, France and the United States established the Federal Republic of Germany, also known as West Germany; the Soviet Union then created the Democratic Republic of Germany in the Eastern Part of the country. This Soviet-occupied East Germany was half the size of West Germany, and included the states of Mecklenburg, Brandenburg, Lusatia, Saxony, and Thuringia. Berlin, the former capital, was split into half Communist East and half free West. Wilhelm Pieck was East Germany's first president, and Otto Grotewohl was the prime minister.

East Germany was dissolved soon after the Berlin Wall fell on November 9, 1989. As the Soviet Union collapsed, Germany's two halves were reunited as a free country on October 3, 1990.

Life was hell during East Germany years under the Soviets, and during recovery from World War II, Herman says.

Since their home and farm were destroyed in the war, members of the Haenert family moved in with some friends: the Greusing family, who lived in the same settlement and lost a son to the war. Herman and Horst contributed work to the Greusing and family farm while attending school. Meanwhile, Herman's parents started the difficult task of rebuilding the three-section family home that included a barn for the animals and a storage room for hay and grain and straw.

"Because of the war – everything was destroyed, so it was very, very difficult to obtain building material," Herman says, recalling hand-mixed mortar. "Everybody pitched in and helped."

People cut logs from harvested timbers and used hand saws to fit the logs to size; then, they would build the framework of the buildings. Due to the lack of roofing material, reed was used in place of shingles. During a topping-out celebration, one of the workers slipped and fell from the roof - a real scary moment for Herman to witness. At that point in time, unlike big cities like Berlin, no indoor plumbing was available in rural areas. Outdoor toilets were the norms, and people used washtubs for bathing and general personal care.

Herman, now in the second grade, and Horst attended classes at a one-building schoolhouse that housed students up to the eighth grade. Herman's mother thought he seemed unchallenged with his grade level.

"She said, 'Well, you're so bored in school. It's not interesting to you because you know everything. Why don't you ask your teacher to put you in third grade?'"

Indeed, Herman skipped ahead a grade. But what he and all the other kids learned was heavily filtered through a lens of Communist propaganda.

Indoctrination

The German school children took Russian-language classes, and all of his school's textbooks had a Communist slant, Herman recalls. Meanwhile, Communist control started dividing neighbors and friends, who didn't know whom to trust. Many people were spying on others.

"Before this happened, your neighbor may have been a very good friend - but not anymore, because they'd become informants to the local Communists."

The suffocating environment made it very difficult to survive. If East German citizens didn't express support for the Communist leadership and spoke out against it, they risked harassment and even imprisonment; Herman's father once went to jail. East Germans could not have any newspapers or magazines from western countries or consume any media from the outside. Even listening to West Berlin radio station RIAS (Rundfunk im Amerikanischen Sektor), which provided news to the Berlin area during the Cold War, was grounds for arrest. People learned not to share much about their lives with their neighbors, because they didn't know who the informants were.

During the 1930s under Nazi rule, German children joined the Hitler Youth organization. Now, under Communist rule, the indoctrinating youth group was called the "Junge Pionere" ("Young Pioneers" in English). Most East German kids ages 6 to 14 joined the well-organized Junge Pionere, which began in December of 1948. They wore blue and held marches and after-school meetings.

"They started at a very young age to teach Communist ideals and everything connected with it," Herman says.

Membership in the Junge Pionere was technically voluntary, but the peer pressure was strong: Kids who didn't join the group became outsiders and were ostracized, and their parents looked suspicious. But Herman's parents refused to let him join the Junge Pionere. The denial may have hurt at the time for a boy who wanted to fit in with his peers, but now, Herman is grateful for it.

"Absolutely, you were an outsider," he says. "When you try to get into sporting groups and all those different things, they reminded you of that."

The Haenert family fell under suspicion because they wouldn't let their sons join the Junge Pionere; few kids opted out. Herman felt lonely, but he coped thanks to having "strong-willed parents who tried to impress on me that this is not the right thing."

Between 1946 and 1952, the family looked forward to care packages their American friends – namely, the Hesselbacher family in Illinois, and Carl and Carrie Dogs in Wisconsin - would send. The delight of a package helped them cope with life. Meanwhile, Herman's Uncle Willie, who lived in West Berlin, was able to make occasional visits via bicycle or train, and he would bring the family food that was not available in East Germany.

After a few years of living under the Soviets - who allowed no private property and took over agriculture – the Haenerts realized their future in Germany would be miserable, and they wanted to immigrate.

"My parents absolutely saw no future in being there, even though they had rebuilt their home," Herman says. "The Communists took land. You were doing the same work, but the government owned it."

Farming families like the Haenerts provided much of their own food, by growing crops and butchering animals. They could only sell whatever was left over after they gave the mandated amount of crops, like potatoes, to the government. Herman's mother planted and maintained a large garden. Among many fruits and vegetables, she grew a specialty - white asparagus, which is still Herman's favorite vegetable.

Herman's parents and big brother Carl, seeing the proverbial writing on the wall, made plans to escape from their Russian-occupied native Germany in 1952. Herman was just in eighth grade.

Chapter 4

Escaping from East Germany

Young children aren't known for secret-keeping abilities; therefore, Herman's family left him and brother Horst out of any discussions about plans to escape East Germany, lest he leak something to the wrong people. These discussions happened among Erich, Tosca and Carl; the younger boys learned of the escape plan the day the family left.

Carl had an edge in escaping East Germany, because he was born in the United States and technically was an American citizen. While visiting his Uncle Willie – his father's cousin - in West Berlin, Carl made contact with the American Consulate there to get his immigration paperwork started. He wanted to take his family with him back to America.

But getting approval from the Americans was the easy part. Even if they would say "Yes," the Communist leaders in East Germany would emphatically say "No." Citizens could not leave their prison-like country, so they had to plan an escape if they wanted to move to a free country.

Sneaking Away

In 1951, Carl bought a train ticket to ride from Ramin to Kahlwinkel, his father's birth place, to make it believable to the authorities in the event of a search. This journey included a stop at a train station in East Berlin, where Carl and other people wanting to escape to freedom would sneak away into West Berlin.

When Carl successfully broke free from East Germany, the leaders put a scope of suspicion on the Haenert family, seen as risky potential escapees. Meanwhile, as East German citizens continued to leave the Communist country for the west, the leaders erected the Berlin Wall to keep them in.

The Haenert family secretly communicated about their escape plans with Uncle Willie through a secret code they used in mailed letters. It was the only way of communicating, since there were no phones at the time – and even if there were, the phones surely would have been wiretapped. Likewise, Communists monitored the mail of East German citizens who received mail from the West, via a clever method of opening envelopes, reading the contents and sealing them again, Herman recalls. But the Haenerts figured out a way around it, though Herman doesn't remember what their codes were; this is one of many questions Herman wished he had asked his Dad and Mother.

"My parents and my Uncle Willie had established certain key words and certain key phrases that would indicate things were progressing," Herman says. "Through pre-arranged communications, basically from Uncle Willie to us, my folks then planned our escape."

A Rebel's Train Trip

Herman had no idea that an escape from East Germany was in the planning stages. Some of the things he wanted to do met with opposition from his parents.

Meanwhile, young Herman had the bright idea that he would travel around Germany to visit relatives all by himself. It took a while to convince his parents to let him do this, but they finally relented and gave permission. At the age of 12, he boarded a train in Grambow - the nearest train station to Ramin - and rode to Berlin, spent some time with Uncle Willie and Aunt Angnes and then to Naumburg to visit his Aunt Ellie and Uncle Gerhardt. They had given him directions on how to get to their place from the train station. He still remembers walking up many steps on the side of the hill to get to their place.

"I guess I was always an entrepreneurial rebel," Herman says. "I wanted to do this by myself, which I did."

After Naumburg, Herman went to his mother's hometown, Mertendorf, and spent a week or so there working on the Kunze family farm with his Uncle Walter. Then, Herman went on to Kahlwinkel, his father's hometown. There, his father came to visit his sister, named Tosca like his wife; this Tosca was celebrating 25 years of marriage to her husband, Hugo Senger. After celebrating the couple's anniversary, Erich took his adventurous 12-year-old son back to Ramin. Herman believes that his father shared his escape plan with his brother Konrad, who resided on the homeplace. The "final Auf Wiedersehen" elevated his suspicions.

West Berlin

The family carried out a covert plan for an escape carrying only one suitcase for each family member, and paper money in their socks, as bank transactions would be traceable. They had to leave everything else behind, including their dairy cows, horses, chicken and geese. They designated a trusted neighbor – Gerhardt Bonin, the only one who knew of their plans - to care for the animals and take over the farm. Herman remembers walking a few miles to the post office box to mail a letter to Mr. Bonin with the family's instructions. Unfortunately, the Communists took over the farm and wouldn't let him have it.

Secrecy and avoiding suspicions were crucial, Herman recalls.

"The plan had to be that there was nothing unusual that we could make any noises of any kind that would be different than everyday living."

One day, around 3 p.m., Herman's father took his mother and Horst to the railroad station in Grambow, where they bought a ticket to Kahlwinkel. At the stop in Berlin, where they were supposed to change trains, Tosca and Horst walked out through the entrance into West Berlin. It was a nerve-wracking and risky journey, as Communist train conductors and station guards questioned passengers. They would observe people closely, examine their paperwork, and interrogate them about where they are going.

After dropping off Tosca and Horst, Erich and Herman returned home. That evening, they milked the cows, put the usual daily milk cans out so their home didn't look suspicious, and then left at midnight for their own escape. They walked through seven miles of timber with suitcases in hand, then boarded a train in Löcknitz. The train stopped in Pasewalk, where Erich worried that his son had disappeared during a bathroom trip – but, they found each other and quickly boarded the train to Berlin on time.

In an age long before cell phones, Erich and Herman did not know whether their family, hours ahead of them, had made it into West Berlin successfully. Meanwhile, they had to be very careful not to look suspicious. They told officials they were going on vacation to Kahlwinkel.

Their cover story and escape plan worked, and Erich and Herman made it into the freedom of West Berlin after their train stopped at the Berlin station. A grateful Uncle Willie met them on the street, and then took them to his apartment.

"Once we got across there, we were on safe ground," Herman recalls. "I remember distinctly there was a big old fruit stand there. I'd never had an orange in my life; there were no oranges in East Germany."

Now that the whole Haenert family had made it to West Berlin, they went to the American consulate to finalize the paperwork authorizing immigration to the United States, where Carl was waiting for them. They encountered an unexpected obstacle: American officials allowed Erich and Tosca to go to America right away, but they required the kids to wait an additional six weeks due to a paperwork glitch.

"My parents said, 'Well, what are we going to do with these boys?'" Herman says.

They found a temporary solution in a boys' orphanage through Johannesstift, a community-service agency run by the Lutheran church. Erich and Tosca left Germany in September of 1952, and left their sons with the church's home for what they thought would be no more than a month and a half. But the wait turned out to be much longer than expected.

The Orphanage

At Johannesstift – where ministries included a nursing home, a home for children with disabilities, and other charitable services – Herman and Horst lived with 20 boys who had lost one or both parents in the war. Caring Lutheran leaders ran the home very well, says Herman, who remains Lutheran to this day.

Horst, then 18, passed the time by learning to become a cabinet-maker - while Herman, then 13, attended "Hochschule," the German form of high school. All boys at the orphanage had many daily duties in the house, like washing dishes, helping with meal preparation, fixing holes in their socks, ironing clothes, and other tasks. They studied the Bible every day, and the kids rang the church bell in the tower every morning. Herman carved his initials into the bell tower, and they are still visible today.

"It was a quick learning experience," Herman recalls.

One boy, Otto Ruthenberg, is still keeping in touch with Herman in 2018. Otto, who lost both his mother and father in the war, grew up to become the director of the Berlin Philharmonic Orchestra Chorus.

Though the initial estimate was a six-week delay, Herman and Horst ended up staying in Berlin without their parents for an entire year. Uncle Willie would visit the brothers regularly, but Horst and Herman mostly felt alone during that difficult year.

"We basically grew up in a hurry, because of all the hiccups in the paperwork process," Herman says.

Congressman Leo E. Allen of Galena, Illinois, stepped in to help expedite the process. Finally, in September of 1953, the boys departed from Berlin's Tempelhof Airport, where the 1948-1949 Berlin Blockade had taken place. In this Cold War event, the Soviets blocked Western allies' access to sectors of Berlin under Western control.

On that note, a few months before their departure for America, Herman and Horst witnessed the June 1953 uprising in East Berlin, from the West Berlin side. Workers demanding economic reforms went on strike, and demonstrations happened in major industrial centers. The Volkspolizei and the Soviet Army suppressed the uprising with tanks, etc. The workers' only ammunition were rocks and shovels and other projectiles, since guns had been confiscated during the Nazi rule.

At Tempelhof Airport, the boys stood in front of this big airplane with an overwhelming sense of awe.

"I was standing there with great anticipation about my first airplane ride, leaving Germany and coming to the new frontier," Herman says.

"We were going to America - the land of opportunity, where money grows on trees and everyone was rich," he says. "That was kind of the impression everyone had."

Herman felt no sadness or mixed feelings, even though they were leaving their native country. All Herman could feel was excitement about going to America, which looked like the Promised Land, and reuniting with his family, after living for a year in a limbo-like situation. He got to escape the prisonlike environment of East Germany, although he feared a possible strike on the plane.

At Tempelhof Airport, the brothers boarded a flight with Sabena World Airlines, which took them to Brussels, Belgium. Due to a late departure that ended up a life-saving twist of fate, Horst and Herman missed their connecting flight to Galway, Ireland. That missed plane crashed.

Once they got to Galway, the boys flew to Newfoundland – and from there, they flew to New York City's Idlewild Airport, which later became John F. Kennedy International Airport; there, officials confiscated a bouquet of roses that Aunt Agnes had given the boys to take to their mother. They looked out the window and checked out the vast expanse of lights from the Manhattan skyline. The city looked so mysterious and glamorous compared to Berlin, which had no high-rise buildings and was still in ruins in many places.

The boys had to transfer to New York's La Guardia Airport for their final flight to Chicago. They had a big problem: They had to figure out how to get from Idlewild to La Guardia without knowing a word of English. The boys took their airplane tickets and pointed out their connecting flight to a couple of people who looked like they knew their way around. As luck would have it, a couple took the boys outside the terminal and put them on the La Guardia bus. With great anticipation, Horst and Herman landed on September 15 at Chicago Midway Airport; there, their parents and Carl met them and brought them out to the farm where they lived. Everyone wept during the ecstatic reunion between two kids, their parents and their older brother, separated by an ocean for one very trying year.

The entire flight journey, happy though the occasion may have been, was difficult and frightening for the German-speaking kids because of language barriers, but many kind people helped them on their way.

Herman recalls a memorable car trip from Chicago to the new family home in Scales Mound in Carl's 1952 green Pontiac. Members of the excited family talked nonstop at once, as they tried to wrap a year of absence into a joyous reunion. They stopped about halfway through the trip at a gas station, where Herman saw and drank his first Coca-Cola. The cold bubbly treat was delicious.

The family returned to the same big farmhouse where Erich and Tosca had lived during the 1920s.

A new American adventure was to begin.

$Chapter$ 5

Settling in to American Life

Herman and Horst moved into their parents' house on the 361-acre Hesselbacher farm – the same house where their parents had lived in the 1920s in Scales Mound, Illinois. The boys each had his own bedroom – a luxury after the Berlin orphanage, which housed two to three kids per room. They felt like they had landed in an American paradise – and compared to life under Communism, it was.

"So now, you wake up and you're out in the country on a big old farm, with many buildings and livestock," Herman recalls.

The Haenert family had financial obligation to repay: The Hesselbachers had paid the boys' and parents' travel expenses to come to America. As soon as they arrived, all family members started working hard to pay back the money by doing farm chores. Horst secured a job working on the Irvin White Farm in Apple River, Illinois - a neighboring community. Herman would milk cows in the morning and help with planting and harvesting. The repayment process took about three years. Meanwhile, Carl – who had bought the farm from his father-in-law – was drafted into the American Army.

The Scales Mound community was so warm and welcoming; it made the family's life and the beginning of our new American home an easier transition. The anticipation of all new surroundings, and the great opportunities of the land of the free, have become a reality.

Herman, Horst and his parents came to America with one suitcase each, carrying their valuables and only belongings - and very little money.

Prior to Herman's parents arrival in Scales Mound in 1952, the Hesselbacher family organized a neighborhood appeal for household items to set up housekeeping for the Haenert family in the farm house. The generous outpouring and caring support of the Scales Mound community provided the family with everything needed including furniture, appliances, dinnerware, and miscellaneous items. Their generosity and outpouring of support will never be forgotten.

Soon after arriving in America, Herman began his adventure as an American high-school student who, at first, knew no English. Herman was somewhat reluctant to start school without knowing one word of English. He also knew that he was going to be looked at as that kid from Germany.

Scales Mound High School

Like all his peers in the same grade at the tiny school, Herman was a freshman – he was pushed back a year from his grade in Germany - and new to Scales Mound High School. Yet there was a major divide: The other kids were English-speaking Americans, and Herman spoke only German.

Before starting classes at Scales Mound, which had only 90 students, Herman's parents along with his sister-in-law Jean, took him in to meet Principal Barnhard. They explained that Herman couldn't speak any English, but they wanted him to attend school there anyway. At the time, schools had no ESL (English as a Second Language) program, so Herman could only learn through total immersion in the day-to-day life of English speaking. He learned by going to movies, listening to the radio, watching TV, learning to read, and asking people questions about what English words meant. He also learned to read body language with smiling, hand signals and the shaking of head and shoulders – meaning someone either approves or doesn't understand.

During Herman's first day in algebra class, the teacher wrote out a math problem – numbers being a universal language - on the chalkboard.

"I couldn't speak a word of English, but I went up to the board and solved the problem," recalls Herman, who already had taken algebra and geometry in Germany. "My classmates were saying, 'Who in the heck is this kid? What does he know?'"

The first year of high school was very rough, with the language barrier. But Herman made friends through playing basketball on the school's team. He loved the sport that was new to him; in Germany, soccer was king and there was no basketball. Herman's basketball coach, Bud Reed, was an influential person in his young life. Herman was co-captain of the basketball team during his senior year along with his friend, Wayne Hickman.

Herman also became interested in running: Scales Mound had no cross-country team, so he became a one-guy team. Even with a cast on an arm after breaking his wrist in basketball, Herman was determined to run a cross-country meet in Rockford, Illinois. He came in 13th out of 150 kids in the regional meet during his junior year.

Through his sports participation, Herman continued to make friends. He recalls a friend named Wayne Hickman, who is still a good friend today. Wayne and Herman got into a lot of trouble together, with common teenage mischief like drinking, fast cars and whatever else they could get into. Cletus Winter was another good friend of theirs; unfortunately, Cletus died a number of years ago.

"For the most part," Herman recalls, "the kids were welcoming."

But still – trying to learn English and communicate was very difficult. Nobody spoke German, so he had to learn English fast or stumble along.

"I'm trying to be accepted and trying all kinds of stuff in this totally different world, and dealing with the language barrier," Herman says. "People look at you. You never know what people felt; I can understand that."

Herman managed to learn major English skills despite the lack of special classes and a German-English dictionary. He passed all his classes, even English, with the help of a teacher, Mrs. Flanagan, who took him under her wing; later in high school, Herman even helped teach a freshman math class. One especially difficult thing about English was learning the words that had multiple meanings. Still, by the end of his freshman year, Herman was pretty proficient in English, and his sophomore year was much easier. He participated in many school activities, including the class plays and singing in the school chorus.

Amazingly, Herman learned to speak English in a fully American style with no German accent, even though the rest of his family had thick accents.

"I had the ear for the language," he says. "Some of the words that were hard to pronounce - I really practiced them."

Academically and socially, life in America was really progressing for Herman, who participated in many fund-raising activities to pay for one of the best highlights of high school: the senior class trip to Washington, D.C. And what a life-changing trip it was.

Washington, D.C.

A group of 12 girls and six boys boarded a bus in Scales Mound for the trip to the nation's capital, chaperoned by science teacher Mr. Hill, who did not understand the meaning of fun. Mr. Hill gave Herman a fair warning: Either you straighten out, or go home.

One of Herman's class mates, Beverly White, had a pre-arranged date: her boyfriend, Gordon Glasgow, who was in the army and stationed in Washington, D.C. Gordy came to visit Beverly at their hotel in D.C. over Mr. Hill's objections. As the word spread that Gordy was visiting Beverly, Mr. Hill did a room check to find Gordy. Little did the teacher know that Herman had hidden Gordy in a closet!

The highlight of the class trip was the meeting with Representative Leo Allen, the congressman who assisted Herman's and Horst's immigration to the U.S. And coincidentally, during a visit to the Tomb of the Unknown Soldier at Arlington National Cemetery, Herman spotted German Chancellor Konrad Adenauer during a guard-changing ceremony.

"During that trip, I was moved by the sacrifices of the many that were buried there, and the price they paid for freedom and for all fellow Americans," says Herman, who climbed the nearly 900 steps to the top of the Washington Monument with his friends. "At the time, I was not an American citizen, but I certainly felt the pride of being one."

The visit to D.C. had a poignant effect on Herman, who didn't know much about American history beyond the classroom in high school. As a young man who had immigrated from Germany, he felt amazed and humbled by the history of his new country – which was much younger than his European homeland.

"I stood there in awe of what it is all about," he says. "Certainly, that helped inspire me to become an American who is going to defend and do all the things that American citizens are going to do - what we are moved to do, born to do."

High school was full of exciting, life-changing growth experiences like this visit to Washington – and, the day a pretty, young new student from Mount Carroll, Illinois, moved to town during his junior year.

Judy

Herman spotted this young lady, Judy Breed, walking down the hallway and thought: "Jesus, that's a good-looking gal!"

"I thought, well, someday maybe I can get a date with her or something," he says.

Years later, Judy would become Herman's wife. But the romance didn't start in high school; they just got to know each other as classmates. Ironically, Judy's uncle – her mother's brother – was dating a Hesselbacher girl.

Judy, with her dark hair and blue eyes, was a "damn good-looking girl and still is." She was very shy and quiet – the opposite of her future husband, who has never been shy or quiet.

Herman graduated in 1957 from Scales Mound High School as the Secretary of his class; and, he had been Vice President of his Junior Class. Most of his peers in the farming community stayed in the area and didn't go to college, but Herman, thinking he would become a coach and math teacher, got two scholarship offers: one from Northern

Illinois University in DeKalb, and the other from Platteville State Teachers College, now the University of Wisconsin-Platteville.

But he didn't accept any of these offers and go straight to college. Herman had some exploring to do first.

Chapter *6*

College and Young Adulthood

After graduating from Scales Mound High School, Herman felt undecided about how to begin his adult life. Should he go to college, or get a job? Or maybe both?

Initially, Herman and his friend, Wayne Hickman, took jobs in Dubuque, Iowa, where they worked at Farley & Loetscher Manufacturing Company building wooden tabletops.

"Deep down, I didn't know exactly what I wanted to do for sure," he says.

Wayne and Herman carpooled the 30 miles to their daily job, where they punched a clock and started working in an assembly-line style at the factory. He would use electric saws with minimal safeguards to cut out tabletops all day. During this job, which only lasted about four months, Herman learned a lot about the union culture and didn't like what he saw from the bosses and the working environment.

Workers had a set number of products to make and couldn't exceed that number per union rules. Companies did not pay bonuses for hard work. Workers in this environment weren't motivated to achieve, and Herman felt limited.

"In my opinion, I want to excel, and I want to be the best – and that was totally discouraged," he recalls. "It was totally different than the work environment in Germany: You achieve, and you keep achieving, and you're driven to achieve.

"To be the best - that is kind of built into you," Herman says about German values.

Herman and Wayne were laid off from Farley & Loetscher and he thought about going to college, but he wasn't sure where he'd get the money. He went to work on the farm of Fred Winter, who is the father of his friend, Clete. Herman performed menial farming tasks like shoveling manure in the dairy barn; meanwhile, he dreamed about a successful life with a wife, kids, and a more intellectual career.

College, Marriage, and Citizenship

During his time in Dubuque working in the factory, Herman wasn't in touch with Judy; she still lived with her parents on the farm in Scales Mound. And that is where he later re-connected with his childhood crush, while driving through his hometown.

"There on the corner of the corner café, stood Judy," Herman recalls fondly. "I stopped and talked to her, and as she tells the story, she picked me up and took me for a ride. I hopped in the car with her – and that's how it all began."

Herman's new romance with Judy led him to his college destination. When the couple reconnected, Judy had been in the process of enrolling at Rockford Business College in Rockford, Illinois. Wanting to be near Judy – and, remembering teachers from high school who really encouraged him to go to college – Herman checked out the school, but didn't know how he would pay for it. Through working three jobs, Herman could cover the college costs – about $1,000 a semester, which was a lot of money at the time - so he enrolled in Rockford Business College with his sweetheart.

While tending to his studies, Herman juggled part-time jobs pumping gas for minimum wage – about $1 an hour at the time - at the Hal's Sinclair station, and typing freight bills for Liberty Trucking Company. He also worked on weekends back at the family farm in Scales Mound – about 75 miles away from Rockford. Meanwhile, Judy worked at Bishop's Cafeteria, and at the Rockford Women's Club.

"On weekends, we both visited our parents," Herman reminisces. "The great thing about going home on weekends was that our parents provided us with a lot of food items for the following week. We always loaded up and made sure we had something."

In Rockford, Herman and Judy each stayed in the school's family housing, where Herman had a roommate named Chuck Rand. Herman studied accounting, and Judy studied to be an executive secretary. Herman inherited his flair for numbers from his father, who worked as an accountant as well as a farmer. He felt like he had chosen the right course of study, and he graduated with an accounting degree in two years.

"Any business needs to have good accountants and good attorneys; these are some of the basics of running a successful business," Herman says. "That's what kind of drove me. Also, if you're involved with the accounting world, you have a very good feel for the business."

Herman's time at Rockford Business College cemented his future career and his personal life with Judy. The happiest day of Herman's life was when he married the love of his life on August 23, 1959, at Zion Lutheran Church in Schapville, Illinois - not far from Scales Mound.

The couple married on a hot Sunday night, after the groom spent a rowdy afternoon on the family farm drinking beer with his buddies including roommate Chuck Rand - who later became the sheriff of Boone County, Illinois – and Wayne. Herman rode a motorcycle on a hidden road, and the bike tipped over; he did not get injured, but still, this wasn't a very good beginning to a wedding day. Meanwhile, the guys tried to smuggle some beer into the back of the church before the ceremony.

When Herman arrived at the church, he discovered that the candles had melted and flopped over. That is what happens on a hot August day before people had air conditioning!

"Everybody had to scramble to find candles," Herman recalls. "That was something that you just don't ever forget."

More than 100 people packed the small country church to watch the bride and groom exchange vows, then went into the church basement for the reception. Herman and Judy borrowed his brother's car for the honeymoon, and Horst conspired with some other people for a newlywed prank: They planted pungent Limburger cheese under the hood, on the 1959 black Chevy Impala's manifold. It reeked, but the newlyweds couldn't deny that the prank was clever and funny.

Despite not having much money or a place to live yet, the couple did manage a short honeymoon to the Milwaukee and Fon Du Lac areas of Wisconsin, with some financial help from family and Horst's car.

"Going on a honeymoon with $49 in your pocket is not a big honeymoon," Herman says.

Herman and Judy still had a year left to go in college, so they had to find their first apartment in Rockford and furnish it with the help of both parents, who provided furniture and a 6-inch TV set, which Herman jokingly calls "huge." They were grateful for whatever they could get. The apartment was on the second floor of Church Street in Rockford, and the apartment shared a bathroom with another building tenant.

"We were in love and are still in love, so you can adjust to whatever one has to," Herman says about his wife. "We made the best of it."

The wedding wasn't the only huge, life-changing event of 1959. That same year, both Herman and his brother, Horst, became American citizens in a ceremony held at the federal courthouse in Freeport, Illinois. They became official, naturalized American citizens at the historic place that once hosted the second Lincoln-Douglas debate in 1858.

This ceremony, attended by family and friends, marked a very proud moment for Herman.

"We had to answer a lot of questions about the constitution, and we were quizzed about American history," he says. "It was a feeling you'd never forget."

Herman is thankful every day for the opportunity of becoming an American citizen.

Chapter 7

Babies, Businesses and Houses

As newlyweds in Rockford, Herman and Judy lived very busy lives. Herman still was working three jobs and finishing up his accounting degree. They didn't have much leisure time except for an occasional movie and evening at McDonald's, where hamburgers – about 80 percent bun and 15 percent meat, as Herman recalls – cost just 15 cents.

A real treat was going to Bishops Cafeteria, where Judy worked, and loading up on everything they could stack onto their plate plus more.

Owning a newer reliable car was a luxury at the time, and families were lucky to have just one vehicle. Herman and Judy drove many old clunkers – that's all they could afford - until Judy found a newer, reliable 1950-something Ford.

Just a few months into their marriage, the Haenerts got a surprise: Judy thought she was pregnant, and indeed, she was. Judy continued to see her German family doctor – Dr. Schlecht, located about 60 miles from Rockford in Elizabeth, Illinois – and she had medical problems, like stomach upsets, throughout the pregnancy. Judy ended her study program, and she moved in with her parents in Apple River during the last six weeks of pregnancy to be close to her doctor.

On July 27, 1960, baby boy Hans Jay – the first of two kids – greeted the world, after some 20 hours of labor. Judy didn't return to school, and she became a stay-at-home mom. Hans "Jay" uses mostly his middle name and looked a little like his father: a blonde German boy.

"Becoming a father was a lot of happiness and a lot of anticipation, and gave me more drive to succeed," Herman says.

Meanwhile, Herman had graduated with an accounting degree in February of 1960, and landed his first professional job at a furniture company.

Hanley Furniture Company

All people remember their first real job following graduation with a degree in hand. It's a definitive time in one's life, and a proud moment. It makes you reflect back to all the part-time jobs, which have the same basic principles and benefits: the value of hard work, increased self-confidence, and self-sufficiency.

"That first job sets the tone for your entire career," Herman reflects.

Young graduates are ready to take on the world, with just one problem: no job experience. It is a huge transition from textbooks and classroom settings to real-world challenges and opportunities. Thankfully, Herman found a wonderful first career job with a Rockford store called Hanley Furniture Company, where he replaced the previous accountant.

"It's hard for a young guy to come into an established firm and say what's happening," Herman says. "You come with a degree in hand, and you leave the textbooks on the shelf."

Still, things worked out very well. At this family-owned company with about 20 employees in downtown Rockford, Herman began a job that would last nine years. He did a lot of analytical work to get a good feel for the business, along with daily accounting practices. Lots of ideas were swirling around his curious and futuristic mind.

In those days, the spreadsheet was a columnar sheet, which accountants drew out with a sharp pencil and eraser. After filling many wastebaskets with sheets of papers full of numbers and ideas over a 12-month period, Herman finally put an analysis of the business in front of the general manager, Oscar Stried, and the owner, David Kupperman. Herman made his analysis based on the history of Hanley Furniture's constant borrowing, resulting from financing all the accounts receivables and assuming all the collection risks and the impact of cash flow.

"You sell something for $300, and it takes you two or three years to get your money back," he says.

A key to the new business plan was selling accounts receivables at a discount to Aetna Finance, which helped Hanley's cash flow since it didn't have to wait for customer payments to come in quickly enough to fund the business. Herman also put a plan together that had customers automatically finance their purchases through Mercury Finance, and he initiated an insurance plan that would cover the payments of customers who become disabled and unable to work. All these elements of the plan removed the risk of Hanley carrying the receivables, and they improved the company's cash flow. Herman's plan was a tough sell to the management, though, as the company feared losing contact with customers if they sold accounts to a third party.

"I felt very excited and so driven. I wanted to make a difference and come up with ideas to make more money for the company and sustain its future," Herman recalls fondly. "I kept coming up with more ideas how to do it and how not to do it. That's a challenge in any job."

Hanley Furniture, located on Main Street, carried more than furniture in its five floors of display and warehousing Like a mom-and-pop version of a Sears, the company carried household appliances, carpeting, and even gifts and jewelry. The store was open seven days a week, and Herman worked half-days on Saturdays and sometimes Sundays.

Herman was well-rewarded for his initiatives and hard work, which paved the way to purchasing their first home on Jonathan Avenue in Rockford. This was another milestone and the realization of the American dream of "homeownership." This house provided Judy and Herman a great starter home for their young family.

He used the finished basement as an office for his side business: doing people's income taxes. Herman also got involved with additional business ventures outside of his job at Hanley, including investing in stocks and trading commodity futures.

He and Oscar, the Hanley manager, started O&H Enterprises, which invested in real estate with the help of attorney Milton Fischer. They teamed up with some other business people in Rockford and bought a historic Rockford building called the Lafayette Hotel, which they converted into apartments. The remodeling of the hotel provided a lot of business for Hanley Furniture, which supplied the carpeting, appliances and furniture. All apartments were rented furnished. That same group of investors purchased numerous other properties in Rockford.

David personally loaned the Haenerts $25,000 to build their dream home, which they created in the countryside just outside of Rockford after living in apartments and their first home on Jonathan Avenue.

One of those apartments was half of a duplex house, with the Haenerts on the ground floor and Wayne and Carol King on the second floor. The couples became good friends – and then, Wayne and Herman worked together on building the new house. Wayne was an electrical contractor and Real Estate investor and developer and sold the Haenerts the property on Shilo Road.

Herman and Wayne did a lot of the building work themselves. Scab labor – union members who weren't supposed to work outside their jobs but did – filled in the rest of the building tasks, done at night. Wayne built a home in the same area for his family, and he and Herman worked together to build the King home. The five King children and two Haenert children became friends, and they did many fun things like going on camping trips together.

After a year or two of the building process, Herman and his family moved into the one-story, ranch-style brick house in 1967. Herman sold their home on Jonathan Avenue himself. The home on Shiloh Road still stands today.

"I was never driven to sit behind the desk as an accountant," he says. "I got involved in a lot of the marketing and contracts with major builders and remodelers and Real Estate developers. I enjoyed doing that."

Herman also was very active in long-range planning to position the business for long-term survival and success. He wanted to add four stores, forming a geographic circle around the central store in downtown Rockford. This plan made sense, because it would grow the business without costing any extra in advertising and other promotional activities. Oscar and David got excited about the expansion and approved the plan.

Herman found the first site, made an offer, and secured a 90-day option on 25 acres of land outside of Freeport, Illinois to build a new Hanley

Furniture store and develop the site. The site stood along Illinois Route 26, and would be used for the first of the four stores in the plan.

Working with a Real Estate developer in Freeport, Herman identified prospects and contacted them for potential leases using the Hanley Furniture Company as the anchor store - all subject to zoning approval. The development plan would pay for a lot of Hanley's costs, and Hanley would become the owner and developer of the strip mall.

Herman's last two years at Hanley Furniture Company were challenging to him, as many of his new ideas were evaluated but not implemented, including a master plan for growth and survival. The deteriorating downtown location with limited parking was a huge factor impacting growth at that location. The growth was happening on the East side of Rockford.

Herman's plan was to move the business into a developing shopping center on busy East State in Rockford, but the Hanley owner did not accept that idea. Backing out of the Freeport deal was the last straw, so to speak, for Herman. The main reason was that the owner was in his late 70's and had no succession plan. Neither of David Kupperman's children – both successful in their own careers and businesses - had an interest in the furniture business, as the daughter lived in Racine, Wisconsin and the son lived in Waukegan, Illinois.

Sensing that his future was not at Hanley Furniture any longer, Herman started to seek the advice of friends and successful business people to evaluate potential opportunities outside of the furniture business.

The store closed in 1993. Years later, the Hanley building burned and had to be demolished in July of 2017.

Overall, Herman's nine years at Hanley Furniture gave him an opportunity to deploy his entrepreneurial mind and set the stage for futuristic planning and achievements. This was made possible by the owner of the store, who gave him the opportunity to fail. The Hanley years were years of firsts for the Haenert family: building and purchasing a home, and starting a family. The birth of their two children - Hans Jay and Heidi Joy - the purchase of their first home, the building of their second home, and the beginning of parenthood and family, formed a life foundation for future business opportunities and more.

Home Life

The Haenert family grew again in 1963, when Judy gave birth to a baby girl named Heidi. Heidi Joy was born on November 24, 1963 – just two days after President John F. Kennedy was assassinated in Dallas. The day she was born also was historic in its own right: A man named Jack Ruby shot presumed assassin Lee Harvey Oswald on live national television. Judy saw the shooting on TV, then went into labor later that day.

Sadly, Heidi was born with pneumonia, and doctors didn't know if she would make it. Yet after spending seven days in the hospital, Heidi – who looks more like her mother - recovered and went home.

The year 1963 also was the year of the Haenerts' first new car: a Ford Galaxy. Meanwhile, they made many lifelong friends in Rockford- especially at their church, St. Mark Lutheran Church. Herman and Oscar, the Hanley manager, also became good personal friends from their working relationship. Oscar, who loved betting on horses, had quite a lucky streak: He once won $20,000 on a single race at Arlington International Racecourse. Oscar, knowing his friend knew how to crunch numbers, gave him $1,000 and asked him to figure out the taxes. Oscar later went on to win $100,000 in the lottery!

Herman may not have won large sums of money, but his American dream was really unfolding – and, coming from Communist East Germany, no one could appreciate it more.

The next step in his life journey came in 1969, when Herman resigned from Hanley and began a new chapter of life.

Chapter 8

Chicago

The year was 1969, and Herman had resigned from his first career job at Hanley Furniture, where he spent nine exciting and fulfilling years. Leaving that life behind for a new venture was a bit scary, but it was time to move on to the next chapter. Now what?

The first idea for a post-Hanley career came from networking with several Rockford-area business people at The Redwood Restaurant, located next door to Hanley. This was the hangout for politicians, business leaders, and other Rockford movers and shakers. Herman enjoyed many lunches and dinners at Redwood, where the mayor visited a few times a week.

"It was a place to meet to discuss all the world's problems and opportunities, and all different business aspects that happened in the city," he says. "There are a lot of people I met there who are influential and successful business people. I got to pick their brains and find out which direction to go."

Herman got to know Redwood owner Peter Stravos and his son, Peter Jr., and they inspired his next career move. Peter Jr., a student at The

John Marshall Law School in Chicago, held a part-time job working on the trading floor of the Chicago Mercantile Exchange.

The "Merc" was founded as The Chicago Butter and Egg Board, until it changed its name to Chicago Mercantile Exchange in 1919. It provided a platform to trade and hedge contracts on eggs, live cattle, live hogs, pork bellies, etc. The Chicago Board of Trades was the competing exchange, offering the same platform for crops like corn, wheat, oats, and barley.

In 2006, the Chicago Board of Trades and Chicago Mercantile Exchange signed an agreement to merge the two exchanges (CME Group, Inc.); this merger became official in 2007.

With his farming background, Herman was intrigued – and, with a growing desire for change, he decided to try a stint as a commodity representative for the Chicago Mercantile Exchange, using his connections through Pete Jr. In 1969, he began work for a company called Woodstock, which was a member of the exchange.

Driving some 85 miles between Rockford and Chicago every day – until his car broke down, and then he took a bus for the commute - Herman started out as a runner on the floor of the exchange. Those were long days. And financially, the move was very risky: Representatives in this business were independent contractors, had no salary, and lived on sales alone. Herman needed to invest his own money to get started, so he convinced Judy to sell their home and fund his new business with the equity; they then purchased a smaller house on Augustana Drive. Herman also liquidated other assets to get the money.

"I basically went into business for myself. I thought I would go ahead and try it and see how it works," he says. "It was a big sacrifice, but it's kind of like rolling the dice. You roll the dice to see if you can build a business for yourself - a totally different business from what I'd been in.

The whole idea was fueled by the fact that I was somewhat successful in trading commodities."

Herman's job as a runner, which lasted about three months, got his foot in the door, and he learned the business right where the action is. He would take stamped and timed orders – for pork bellies, eggs, cattle, hogs, and more - from businesses. This was an entry-level job that was a necessary step for Herman's higher ambitions: becoming a representative, a job for which he was training while working. This job pays only on commissions, and like with the stock market, money can be made and lost quickly.

"The long-term goal was to be able to buy a seat on the exchange," he says. "It was stressful, especially when you lost people's money."

Herman achieved his goal of becoming a representative, but he grew weary of the business, which wasn't going as well as he had hoped. The daily bus rides back and forth between Chicago and Rockford felt longer and longer, and Herman was tired of it. He knew it was a risky business, but he thought he could make good money. Alas, it didn't work out that way.

"I was not making the money for my customers like I wanted to – I basically said, 'This is a risky business, but I think we can make some money.' In the long run, it became very, very stressful. I soon found out that you have to have very deep pockets to succeed and stay in that business."

Although Herman struggled with regrets over entering the mercantile-exchange business, he had no regrets about leaving his secure job at Hanley. Still, having the security of a full-time job was nice, and the stress of maybe losing everything he'd worked for took its toll on Herman – especially since he had two young children and a wife depending on him. He was doing some side weekend jobs with his friend Wayne King, but he was struggling to make ends meet.

"Things were not going as I had anticipated, and I was getting pretty frustrated," he recalls. "There are a lot of people in that business who make a lot of money and lose a lot of money, but they've got sustainability."

Herman, who had a hard time accepting defeat, went through a painful period of self-examination about his life goals and career. Judy consoled her husband, reassuring him that they will find another path and make it. Though it was a difficult decision, Herman pulled the plug on the exchange business and decided to go in a new direction – one that utilized his accounting and farming background.

Chapter 9

The Animal-Health Business

Having lost most the savings that Herman and Judy had accumulated to start the commodity trading business, he had to set a new path for basic survival. Herman had to quit and face the people who trusted him with funds to invest; but, he had lost at least half of their funds. The clients – some of whom had been good friends - had entrusted him to make a return on their investment, but that didn't happen. The friendships were casualties of this fallout.

However, another friendship led to both a lasting business and personal alliance. Herman and Judy had many good friends St. Mark Lutheran Church - among them, Dr. Allen Joesten, who was also a commodity customer who understood the risks of investing in commodities. He knew Herman was struggling, as Herman communicated with him on a regular basis.

Often, the biggest opportunities and changes in life start with a simple but fateful conversation and meeting. That is what happened to Herman one Sunday morning after church in 1970, when Dr.

Joesten – the Haenerts' veterinarian – came over and said, "If you are not doing anything worthwhile yet, or have any commitments, I would like you to meet me at my farm on Riverside Boulevard and discuss a business opportunity."

The vet knew that Herman was looking at a home-decorating business in Rockford, as an extension of a small carpet and drapery business (J&H Interiors) that Herman had started. Dr. Joesten, however, did not know the status of the negotiations.

Herman and Dr. Joesten, meeting on the former dairy farm, sat down in the old milk house. Allen presented Herman with an opportunity to join him in a start-up business venture called Wholesale Veterinary Supply. He described the idea of a mail-order business selling veterinary supplies directly to farmers, and Allen asked for Herman's opinion. He offered Herman an opportunity to help develop the business, contribute his hard work and creativity, and share in its success. Dr. Joesten worked many hours operating and managing his Hillcrest Animal Hospital – a five-veterinarian practice - on Alpine Road in Rockford, and he had little time to devote to the new venture.

The vet showed Herman the partially remodeled dairy barn, which would be used as a warehouse to operate the brand-new Wholesale Veterinary Supply. Herman, with his background in both farming and business, saw a lot of potential, felt excited, and accepted his friend's offer.

Wholesale Veterinary Supply

During Herman's first day on the job, Dr. Joesten handed him a shoebox full of start-up invoices - paid and unpaid - and said it was time to set up the business' books. Additionally, he handed Herman the checkbook and said, "We need to pay some of those unpaid bills. If there is not enough money in the bank, we need to go to First National Bank, take out a loan, and add your signature to the account."

Allen told Herman that, since he had just come from a gambling business, he should be able to roll the dice with him. Herman did, thus began a new, exciting chapter in Herman's business venture with Wholesale Veterinary Supply and the Animal Health World.

"Instead of having a retail store, the catalog became your store," Herman says. "In those days way back when, farmers bought a lot of their goods through the Sears and Montgomery Ward catalogs. The point is that farmers were used to buying products from catalogs."

Especially with the lack of overhead costs from running a brick-and-mortar business, Herman saw great profit potential – not to mention a ground-floor opportunity, since the animal-health industry for both livestock and pets was in its infancy stage. Also, Dr. Joesten had invested his own start-up money in the business, so Herman only needed to contribute his time and talent rather than risk any remaining savings.

The business started with a 10-page catalog made of inexpensive newsprint, produced and printed at the Belvidere Daily Republican Newspaper in Belvidere, Illinois. The products in the original catalog included products Dr. Joesten used in his large-animal practice. Herman and the vet mailed catalogs to farmers' addresses obtained by purchasing mailing lists from farm publications like the Farm Journal and Dairy Herd Management.

Originally, the business owners targeted a five-state area. They inserted into the catalogs order blanks, which gave customers options including paying by check or COD (cash-on-delivery). The cash-only business was designed to use cash flow to grow the business. They also installed a toll-free number for customers to place orders, which provided a great addition to the catalog marketing.

Orders started coming in from customers via mail order and telephone. They purchased products like antibiotics, penicillin, dewormers, and just about anything else farmers use to keep their animals healthy every day. Farmers had started to do a lot of their own routine animal health treatments, rather than calling their veterinarian.

The people of Wholesale Veterinary Supply and their customers were happy, but veterinarians weren't, because they were selling the same products to customers at higher prices. Dr. Joesten also gave veterinary advice to customers over the phone, which gave the company a competitive edge.

Herman had to learn the catalog business and the animal-health business at the same time. He soon discovered a major issue that would impede future growth: Wholesale Vet's only supplier was a distributor in Springfield, Illinois, and Dr. Joesten purchased products under his name from direct-selling veterinary products manufacturers.

As the business grew, so did the pressure on Dr. Joesten. Other veterinarians soon discovered who supplied Dr. Joesten and Wholesale Vet, and threatened him and Wholesale Vet's suppliers. Local and state veterinary associations voted to expel Dr. Joesten. Herman and Dr. Joesten strategized for the long-term survival of Wholesale Veterinary Supply and Dr. Joesten's veterinary license.

Dr. Joesten did not want to risk losing his license, so he and Herman came up with a short-term solution for survival, and a long-term solution for the growth of the business. The short-term solution was to channel the purchases through another veterinarian (Dr. Joesten's former classmate), establish relationships with animal-health products manufacturers who would sell to Wholesale Vet directly, and find a partner who has product contracts with manufacturers and buys products from them. One possibility was to do a merger and buy out Dr. Joesten.

Herman had been in contact with many animal-health products manufacturers to buy the products directly. He was fortunate in establishing a direct contract with Colorado Serum Company, Anchor Serum, Ideal Instrument, and couple of smaller suppliers. Many other manufacturers turned them down because of the "catalog" direct-sales strategy.

The model they had was futuristic and there was only one catalog competitor in the United States – namely, Omaha Vaccine Company, which was owned by a veterinarian named Bob Asmus. Herman later found out that they wanted to expel him from the vet associations, but good luck with that. Herman told them, "Go to hell and said see you in court!"

Herman's attorney, Milt Fisher, introduced him to fellow attorney by the name of Jim Shelden, who rented an office from Milt and had a company called Cole Chemical, which had locations in Madison, Wisconsin; and Rockford and Springfield, Illinois. As it turns out, although Cole Chemical's basic business was sales and distribution of Agricultural Chemicals, the company also had an animal-health business selling to dealers and feed mills. The animal-health manufacturers in the early '60s started distributing animal-health products through Ag Chemical distributors, because they already had the infrastructure in place to reach the farmers through their dealer networks. Herman and Dr. Joesten established a relationship with Cole Chemical and they became a main supplier of products for their catalog.

As the pressure increased on Dr. Joesten, earnest negotiations began to either merge with Cole Chemical or sell to Cole Chemical. Cole Chemical had merged with Hopkins Agricultural Chemicals in the late '60's to combine their businesses, on the AgChem side and more. Both companies produced a line of fly sprays and rat baits, among many other products produced and sold under the Dr. Roberts label and Crown Chemical..

Herman sat down with Jim to negotiate the sale of Wholesale Veterinary Supply to Cole. It was a good fit for both companies, since Jim already was in the business, and he needed someone else to manage things and grow the animal-health business. Meanwhile, Dr. Joesten took a buyout and left the business to focus on his practice at Hillcrest Animal Hospital, although the company continued to buy certain products from his clinic.

The move from the remodeled dairy barn to the modern Cole Chemical facility was a welcome change for Herman and seven employees. They could actually use a fork lift and modern warehouse racking, and they reduced a lot of labor-intensive, back-breaking exertions.

Herman renamed the Cole Chemical animal-health business to" Cole Animal Health." That business would continue to sell to dealers. Cole had one salesman on the road in Illinois named Paul Vehigly, and three salespeople in Wisconsin. Wholesale Vet would be the direct catalog-sales company. Herman became President of Wholesale Veterinary Supply, and he ran the entire animal-health business.

With all the tools in hand, including adequate capital, the journey to build the business began by working day and night. Jim, an attorney by training, worked with Herman as his business partner. They formed relationships with suppliers and put together a business plan based on the potential in the animal health field. Herman worked on producing the catalog updates and other projects at night; as the business grew, he hired people to work on the production of the catalog. He also hired more people, both into management and warehouse positions. He made most of the hires in advance of the need - including his son, Jay, who started working in the warehouse after his 16th birthday. Herman said our motto was "Every order shipped, same day as received." And he made everyone in the company live by that every day.

Herman was happy to see his business venture growing. The 10-page catalog grew to 74 pages and mailed to every state, three to four times a year. A funny thing happened: As the business grew, the manufacturers now came to Herman asking for Wholesale Vet to carry their products, Herman also established a walk-in business; local farmers came in with their shopping lists and purchased products directly from the warehouse.

Wholesale Vet became very active with local, state and national trade associations, which established and cemented relationships with livestock producers and manufacturers. The company exhibited at major shows around the country to link the catalog with faces.

Having adequate capital gave Herman the opportunity to buy in volume and negotiate great deals on specialty products. The company set new sales records every day, hired more employees, and expanded warehouse space to support the growth.

It was time to hire a general manager to work directly under Herman. Rich Shuler, a sales representative for the Upjohn Co., had always impressed Herman, so he called on him. Herman hired Rich and moved his family from Kalamazoo, Michigan to Rockford.

Having hired a general manager, Herman laid out a new plan and presented it to Jim Shelden. His plan was to establish a separate catalog for the growing companion-animal market serving pets like dogs and cats and horses; later, Herman and the team put together a separate catalog for the companion animals and became extremely successful. Additionally, Herman wanted to look at acquisitions, both products and companies; and, explore a really wild and risky idea of forming another company to sell directly to veterinarians.

Jim supported the strategies. He would suck on his pipe while slowly talking to Herman, and say "Well, you seem to know what you are doing. We have come a long ways, and made a lot of money."

The success let Herman and Judy afford to purchase a beautiful home, complete with a 40-20 swimming pool, on Sage Avenue in Rockford. He marveled at how the American dream unfolded with him: Herman went from broke and almost desperate to buying this dream home for the family.

The success of Cole Animal Health and Wholesale Veterinary Supply earned Herman many industry awards. The achievement of purchasing targets from companies like American Cyanamid, Pfizer and Elanco earned meeting trips for Herman and Judy to many exotic places. Their destinations included Hawaii, Mexico City, Cancun, Cabo, Acapulco, Bermuda, Venezuela, UK, Scotland, Belgium, Holland, Jamaica, St. Thomas, Puerto Rico, St. Martin, Bahamas, Hong Kong and many major cities in our own great country. As a great side benefit from all those meetings, he formed many lasting friendships with fellow industry people.

Being very active in the industry, Herman served on the Board of Directors of the American Veterinary Distributors Association (AVDA); his time there included a stint as president and chairman.

While attending different trade shows, Herman got acquainted with a company out of Milwaukee, Wisconsin named Groom Rite. They had a line of grooming products - another target in the business plan - including a unique patented grooming table with adjustable legs. There was nothing else like that on the market. Herman successfully negotiated the purchase of the company, including the Groom Rite name, and moved it to Rockford. He told some of the equipment and two products he did not want to another company, and Herman recouped a major portion of the purchase price.

Under the leadership of Rich Shuler, the company's salesforce increased to cover territories in Iowa and target large feed yards and dairies. Rich also hired summer interns, mostly animal-science students from Iowa State University. Some became full-time employees following graduation. Company leaders decided to close the Madison warehouse and move all the inventory to Rockford, thus eliminating duplications and reducing overhead.

More Businesses

Herman's idea of establishing a company to sell to veterinarians was based on the market potential, as the animal-health market was split 50/50 between veterinarians (referred to as the ethical market) and over-the-counter sales. It would require additional distribution contracts with some of the same manufacturers that were supplying Cole and Wholesale, but with a product line specifically labeled for veterinarians. In some cases, that presented a major obstacle.

To overcome that obstacle, Herman attempted to acquire existing ethical distributors that already had the distribution contracts. But that strategy failed, mostly because the purchase price did not meet the return on investment scale.

Herman created Pro-Vet of Loves Park as a mail-order business to veterinarians modeled on the success of Wholesale Vet. He specifically wanted to associate the City of Loves Park (a community adjacent to Rockford) with Pro-Vet to create a different mailing address than Wholesale Veterinary Supply had. It was a calculated risk that paid off big time; lots of hard work and determination never to give up made Pro-Vet the third leg of stool that Herman had envisioned.

In addition to catalog sales, the company hired sales people to call on the veterinarians in Illinois, Wisconsin, Iowa and Michigan. One of those sales people hired for Michigan was George Rankin, who was the star salesman and later promoted by Herman to become the General Manager of the Animal Health Business. With his new job, George moved to Rockford from Michigan.

Never short on ideas, Herman started another company called "The Discount Doctor," which had catalogs in in a folded newspaper format. It featured discontinued items and discounted specials.

In the early 80's, during Jimmy Carter's presidency, prime interest rates skyrocketed into the 20 percent rate. All businesses that had borrowed funds to run their business were struggling for survival – and the Ag Chemical business, the main business of Hopkins Agricultural Chemicals, was no exception. Margins on Ag Chemicals were extremely low, with the added pressure of very expensive borrowing and the farmer's inability to pay for their chemicals on a timely basis. This called for a survival strategy.

Still, Wholesale Vet and related animal-health companies continued to perform well, despite the financial turmoil.

But the drain of capital caused by mounting losses in the Ag Chemical business necessitated the sale of Hopkins Agricultural Chemical Company and all related businesses to ConAgra. ConAgra had been acquiring Ag Chemical businesses throughout the U.S. under their operating company called United Agri Products (UAP), located in Greeley, Colorado.

The original negotiations excluded the animal-health business, but UAP was going to walk if the most profitable part of Hopkins was not part of the deal. What complicated final negotiations was Jim Shelden's unfortunate fall out of a tree. He landed on his head, which basically left him incapacitated for a long time; and, Jim was the majority shareholder of Hopkins. Fortunately, after years of treatments, Jim recovered to about 90 percent of his previous state of mind.

Herman had to agree to selling Wholesale Vet in exchange for a non-compete contract with ConAgra, a handsome payout, and an earn-out reward based on future performance of the animal-health division. Additionally, Herman was named president of all animal health at ConAgra. Ironically, ConAgra had previously purchased Omaha Vaccine, which was Wholesale Vet's primary competitor. It's funny how things work out.

ConAgra had a pension plan, which would be a great benefit to all Wholesale Vet employees. Herman was able to negotiate the start date for all Wholesale employees back to the starting date with Wholesale, instead of the date of sale to ConAgra.

A new chapter had begun for Herman, who now was a part of a publicly traded company.

Chapter *10*

The Birth of a
New Company

Just like he did at Hanley Furniture many years before, Herman came up with a plan to maximize business growth and profits.

Before and during negotiations on the sale of Hopkins Ag/Wholesale Vet to ConAgra in November of 1984, Herman had an idea he shared with Scott Remington. Scott was a sales representative for Agri-Mart, one of the manufacturers of a wide range of animal-health products sold to Wholesale Vet. Agri-Mart was a division of Tech America, based in St. Joseph, Missouri. This company's founder and president was Wes Remington, Scott's father.

Herman was very concerned that the large distributors were getting better prices from the major animal manufacturers because of large-volume purchasing power, which impacted the smaller distributor's ability to compete or stay in business.

Herman laid out his three-part plan on a legal-sized yellow pad. His first idea was to form a corporation with shareholders that would be small animal-health distributors. The combined purchasing power of a group of smaller distributors, Herman thought, would be greater than any single, major animal-health distributor.

The second part of his plan was to establish a line of animal-health goods as private-label products, bearing the name of the newly formed company and only available to its shareholders. The third part of Herman's plan was to work with a manufacturer that would be interested in investing in the new company and producing the products under private label. That's why Herman shared his idea with Scott and his Dad Wes, who were excited about the plan and wanted to have in-depth discussions about doing business together.

The Beginning of Agri-Labs

On a cold December day in 1983, Scott, Wes Remington, and his right-hand man, John Payne, flew into the Greater Rockford Airport in Wes' private plane to explore the possibilities of the venture. Not to be out-done, Herman hired a limousine and picked the group up at the airport.

The group agreed to the general concept of Herman's idea and decided to contact several current Agri-Mart distributors to confidentially test Herman's brainchild. They each contacted one distributor to basically float the idea and ask if the company was open to investing. The response was overwhelmingly positive.

An exploratory committee formed, and members – including Tech America's legal team - agreed to meet in St. Louis. Tech America would own 51 percent of the shares, and the members and shareholders would own 49 percent. Tech America would fund its share with finished goods inventory, and each of the distributor/shareholders would invest $5,000 each. The committee formed the basic outline of a new corporation called Agri-Laboratories, Ltd. (AgriLabs, informally).

They formed a hit list of 34 possible members/owners that group members could contact.

Out of those 34 companies, 25 agreed to invest in Agri-Labs, and the new company became a reality on August 31, 1984. All 25 companies attended the first organizing meeting held October 15, 1984, at the Marriott Hotel in Kansas City, Missouri. Representatives elected a board of directors and made plans for the first annual shareholder meeting in Nashville, Tennessee.

Herman loved watching his dream become a reality – a journey that held plenty of challenges along the way.

ConAgra Challenges and Opportunities

It is quite an adjustment to transform from an entrepreneur to a leader within a publicly traded company. Herman had to adjust to accurate forecasting, earning calls, shareholder values, stock price and performing, and reporting quarter to quarter.

The public announcement on the sale of Hopkins and Wholesale Vet reverberated throughout the animal-health industry. ConAgra - a rapidly growing, $2-plus-billion-dollar company - now appeared on the radar screen of the animal-health manufacturers, domestically and internationally.

ConAgra required Herman to sign a 5-year commitment/non-compete agreement to grow the animal-health business. Teamwork is very important in results and outcomes, and Herman had a great team. His team included his son, Jay, who was the director of purchasing; Lois Kiefer, chief financial officer (and previous employee for Hanley Furniture Company); George Rankin, national sales manager; Phil Trapp, head of IT; and Dr. Don Bend, head of technical service. They presented a five-year plan to the ConAgra management. This plan included the capital requirements to achieve the goals and a return on invested capital estimation.

The plan called for internal growth by expanding the sales force, territories, product development and offerings, and acquisitions. The plan also included a capital request for a computer system to accommodate the present business and future growth. Herman concluded that mergers and acquisitions are like putting a jigsaw puzzle together: Each piece has a unique place, and understanding this is crucial.

Herman had attended many trade shows and conferences, and he saw a growth potential in premium dog and cat diets. The top-selling brands were Hill's Prescription Diet, Iams, and Eukanuba. Both companies limited distribution and had rigid requirements for distributors to carry their brands. Territories were also restricted, as well as sales to veterinarians only for the Hill's brand.

Pro-Vet Carter

Having failed numerous times to gain distribution rights, Herman shifted strategies and targeted the Carter Company. This business – owned by a Jimmy Carter, but not the American president – was an established, specialty-diet-distribution company in Converse, Indiana. The Carter Company had distribution contracts with both Hill's and Iams.

Negotiations to purchase the business required numerous trips to Converse and meet with Jimmy Carter and his advisors. Negotiations also included meetings with Hill's and Iams to make sure they would transfer the distribution contracts to Pro-Pet of Loves Park, now a ConAgra company.

Herman successfully negotiated the purchase of the Carter Company and moved the business to a new warehouse facility in Kokomo,

Indiana. The new company became Pro-Vet Carter, a full-service distribution business serving veterinarians in Indiana and surrounding areas. Substantial growth necessitated moving the business to a 25,000-square-foot building in Indianapolis, Indiana.

The Iams company granted Pro-Vet permission to stock its product line in Rockford, and to sell both to veterinarians and other outlets. That opportunity gave birth to another one of Herman's ideas: a retail store positioned in the Rockford warehouse. A supplier and friend named Bob Migatz introduced Herman to Jim Dougherty, who had a large pet-products retail store in Las Vegas. Jim later became the founder and owner of PetSmart.

Herman listened and learned about the pet-retail business and opened Rockford Pet and Livestock Supply. The store became very popular, with many TV promotions and on-site radio broadcasts. Loyal and knowledgeable employees contributed to the success of Rockford Pet and Livestock Supply.

Prior to the expansion of PetSmart, the success of the Rockford store gave birth to a plan to open pet retail stores in major metropolitan areas across the U.S. The first one of those stores opened in Omaha, Nebraska under the name of Petfoods, Etc.

Meanwhile, Pro-Vet continued to grow with expanded sales forces. Herman targeted growth in the Northwest, specifically in Seattle, Washington. He targeted an acquisition in Seattle - namely Professional Vet Distributing, owned by veterinarian Dr. Brown. The animal doctor converted an old post office into a "warehousing" operation. Professional Vet serviced veterinarians in Washington and Oregon, and had a nice business established in Japan.

Dr. Brown was a difficult, cantankerous person, which made negotiations especially challenging for Herman. But Doc Brown was always short on cash flow, and Herman's due diligence discovered other interesting situations that he used as negotiating tools. Dr. Brown's son-in-law was his attorney, which added additional drama to consummating a deal.

Finally, after three trips to Seattle, the deal was closed in the son-in-law's office. The ConAgra attorney and Herman had a very interesting closing, as Dr. Brown claimed that the four Seahawks season tickets the company owned belonged to him personally. They finally agreed that Dr. Brown can use two tickets for one year.

After the closing, Dr. Brown told Herman, "I forgot something in the building." Herman said, "What is it? I'll get it for you." The doctor said the toilet paper in each of the bathrooms belonged to him, and he was going to get them." Funny!

Herman promoted David Roe, a successful Pro-Vet salesman in Michigan with a lot of veterinary experience, to manage the new Seattle operation: Pro-Vet of Seattle. The first order of business was to build and lease a new warehouse.

The new venture in the Pacific Northwest blossomed: Pro-Vet of Seattle became a very successful business.

Chapter 11

Southwest Expansion: The Titus Acquisition

Herman's active participation in the American Veterinary Distributors Association (AVDA) formed a foundation for many industry friendships and opportunities - especially merger and acquisition candidates.

That was the case with the Titus Company, located in City of Industry, California. The Titus Company had an animal-health distribution business as well as a human-drug distribution business. California was a target growth territory for the expansion of Pro-Vet, and Herman got interested in looking at Titus as a potential acquisition. He got to know Susi Titus at the AVDA meetings and struck up a conversation with her about their future growth plans. Perhaps, Herman asked, they might have an interest in selling their animal-health business?

As a result of their conversation, Susi invited Herman to come to California and start an initial dialogue about how the companies could work together; and, whether Pro-Vet/ConAgra might buy out Titus Animal Health. Titus was lacking several key distribution contracts, which restricted the company's growth and its ability to be a full-service distributor. Meanwhile, Pro-Vet – with its ownership of Pro-Vet in Seattle and Indiana, and ownership by Fortune-500 ConAgra – had earned distribution contracts from all major animal-health manufacturers.

Titus agreed to Herman's buyout offer and the difficult due-diligence process began, uncovering many obstacles because of intertwining the animal-health business with the human Titus business. Employee issues surfaced, as some worked for both businesses. Additionally, the Titus Company had not complied with all of the state of California's licensing requirements; this necessitated numerous trips to Sacramento to resolve the issues.

Struggling through a highly contentious closing with Titus' California attorneys, Herman was ready to walk away from the deal. But cooler heads prevailed, thanks to mitigation by the ConAgra attorney.

Included in the deal was a lease within the Titus human-business warehouse, and newly remodeled offices. Herman retained all Titus employees and incorporated the Pro-Vet/ConAgra compensation plan. Many rejected this incentive-driven plan, but only one person quit. Pro-Vet Titus became operational.

Susi Titus agreed to stay on for a period of time, for the sake of continuity. Herman hired a highly recommend industry veteran as the general manager – but, this manager turned out to be a bust and had to be fired.

Incorporating a newly acquired entity into an existing company is always challenging, and the Titus acquisition was no exception. Yet, despite all the start–up obstacles, Pro-Vet Titus grew as forecasted. The company opened another location in Hayward, California to provide fast service to the veterinarians in that part of California. Additionally, sales personnel joined the staff to service Arizona from the California warehouses.

On one of Herman's many trips to California, he had an opportunity to be on the set of Roseanne Barr's show. He also had dinner with John Goodman – a meeting arranged by John's good friend, Steve Rankin, whose brother George was Herman's national sales manager.

Market research had shown that Las Vegas was a fast-growing market for a veterinary-distribution business. Herman explored opening a warehouse facility in Vegas but decided against it. That tuned out to be a bad decision, as the market in Vegas grew as forecasted. But, he did expand into another part of the country, farther south and east.

Texas and Oklahoma

Herman's growth and expansion plans targeted Texas and Oklahoma. Donnell Ag - located in Graham, Texas - was a unique acquisition candidate because the company sold both animal-health products as well as specialty chemicals. Donnell Ag had a distribution contract for a specialty chemical that none of the ConAgra /UAP distribution companies had been able to obtain. If Herman's company was successful in purchasing the Donnell Ag Company, the manufacturer of the specialty chemical that killed fire ants would assign the distribution contract to a ConAgra/ProVet company.

That opportunity set the wheels in motion to acquire the Donnell Ag company, which had locations in Graham and other Texas areas, and in Oklahoma City, Oklahoma. Donnell Ag did not sell to veterinarians; the company only sold products to farmers directly and to a dealer network. Herman envisioned incorporating a Pro-Vet distribution business within Donnell Ag to expand the business.

As thing tend to move a little more slowly in Texas, the negotiation to consummate a deal in Graham didn't go quickly. Herman got to know the Dallas-Fort Worth Airport pretty well, and he got used to the drive to Graham. At the time, though, Graham did not have many motel choices, so Herman's first night there was a memorable "buggy motel" experience.

Later, Tommy Donnell found Herman a "bug-free" motel for all future visits – which was good, because the negotiations to acquire Donnell dragged on for some time. Deal terms were difficult, and employee issues, warehouse leases, and valuation of inventories got very complicated. Additionally, any potential environmental issues had to be addressed.

Having overcome all the major obstacles on a give-and-take basis, the business leaders reached a win-win agreement - and Donnell Ag became an operating division of Pro-Vet. Having successfully incorporated the new acquisitions, which came with plenty of challenges, they initiated a new plan of action. ConAgra's objective was to have commanding positions in any of the company's business units, animal health included.

Herman's boss at UAP/ConAgra strategized with Herman, and they reached the conclusion that it takes as much time and effort to acquire small companies as it does to acquire large companies. He committed capital to Herman for funding the large acquisitions, if the return requirements were met.

Positioned with capital and the new strategy, Herman targeted the two largest animal-health distributors: one in the "ethical veterinary channel," and one in the "over-the-counter veterinary channel." Herman personally knew both the owners. Following initial due diligence from both companies, the owners' reluctance to sell - and the non-achievable financial returns, based on their terms - nixed both deals.

But Herman had plenty of other things going on in his life and career.

Extracurricular Activities

Herman was a busy guy. He worked on growing the ConAgra animal-health business, while serving as president/chairman of board of the American Veterinary Distributor Association (AVDA). He also served on the board of AgriLabs, and served as president of Forest Hills Country Club in Rockford.

During his AVDA tenure, he initiated and gained board approval for several major projects. To comply with the Occupational Safety & Health Administration (OSHA) Material Safety Data Sheet (MSDS) requirements, Herman presented a plan to the AVDA members at their conference in San Diego. The plan aimed to establish a clearing house for all members' MSDS documents, and to publish an MSDS manual and updates. The project was successfully completed, and the online version of that project is in use today.

The founding fathers of AVDA were all "ethical distributors," selling products to veterinarians only. Another one of Herman's ideas was to open the organization to all animal-health distributors. Following many discussions, the board approved the bylaw change.

Adrian Bayley - who was the publisher of the Companion, a reference book of all animal-health products – approached Herman to market the Companion through AVDA members; AVDA would receive a commission. The board approved the proposal. Today, through the magic of the internet, the Companion is available online.

Serving on the AgriLabs board was a great experience for Herman, who saw his dream become reality and participated in the growth and progress of the company.

Meanwhile, Herman really enjoyed his memorable time as president of Forest Hills Country Club, which gave him the best preparation for running a business. Having served on the long-range planning committee prior to being elected to the Board of Governors, the committee recommended a major remodeling of the club house and improvements to the golf course. The board approved hiring a country club architectural firm to get a general idea of the scope of the project. The word leaked out, causing a major uproar throughout the membership; the project cost was approximately $2.5 million. The most vocal people were the members with the most money and the more senior people.

Selling the project to the membership fell into Herman's lap. He hired a local TV personality: weatherman Bob Kevern, who also owned a marketing/advertising business. Herman and Bob prepared a slide presentation exhibiting pictures of the 50-year-old boilers that broke down every winter. This exposed potential fire hazards in the kitchen, and potential health-department issues. Herman and Bob introduced the idea of converting the storage area overlooking the pool to an informal-dining area. Despite a lot of opposition to the plan, Herman was able to sell the project, including a unique financing plan, to the members. The fruits of his labor as a past president and board member of Forest Hills Country Club are still visible today.

Herman left a big footprint in Rockford, but he wasn't meant to stay there for life. A new adventure was beckoning the Haenert family out to the desert of Arizona. Before settling out west, though, Herman and his family had a transformative experience when they went back to his homeland to visit Germany, after communism collapsed.

Chapter *12*

The Fall of Communism and a Trip to Remember

Herman had not been back to his home country since he escaped to America in the early 1950s. He couldn't: People who left Communist countries without permission got themselves on hit lists.

But then, in 1989, a miraculous thing happened that drew the world's eyes toward Berlin: On November 9, jubilant people started dismantling the Berlin Wall that had divided the country since 1961 and imprisoned the Eastern part of the city. Tearing down this wall, as President Ronald Reagan had admonished Russian leader Mikhail Gorbachev to do, seemed an unlikely dream to come true – but now, it was happening. The prayers of millions of people had been answered.

When the wall started to come down, Herman was in Italy for a business trip. He called Judy as he does every night during his travels and she said, "Have you seen the news?" Judy said. "The Berlin wall is coming down!!!"

"I was shocked," Herman recalls. "Of course, it was always a hope that someday I could go back to the place I was born. But it seemed very unlikely.

"I was just utterly elated," he said. "The only thing that I felt bad about is that my parents would never be able to see that."

Herman found his mother's old address book with contact information for his lost German relatives (mostly cousins) and friends. They reached out to these people they hadn't seen in a few decades, expressed joy about Germany's tremendous breakthrough, and pledged to come visit. In July of 1990, the couple took that trip back to Herman's homeland.

Back to Germany

Having contacted relatives and friends while planning Herman's return trip to his former homeland, they responded with joy and open arms. Those who had space in their houses were insistent Herman and Judy stay with them in their homes.

The anticipation of going back to the former East Germany to see friends and relatives after 38 years – and, to again visit the places Herman spent his youth, and subject Judy to a totally different culture and language - stirred certain emotions within Herman.

As soon as Herman finished the itinerary for the journey, he mailed a copy to the friends and relatives. None of the friends or relatives in the former East Germany had telephones in 1990.

The first part of this almost three-week journey was to fly to Berlin, where Herman's cousin Troudchen – daughter of Uncle Willie, who helped him escape, and friend Hanjo – greeted them at Berlin Tegel Airport. Since Troudchen's place was very small, Herman and Judy stayed at the Europa Hotel, centrally located in Berlin.

With luggage in hand, Troudchen retrieved her Mercedes from the parking lot, and Herman and Judy were on the way to the Europa Hotel. Troudchen had her own action-packed, four-day itinerary, starting right after the hotel check-in; nobody had time to think about jetlag. Troudchen, born and raised in Berlin, had an awesome historical knowledge of the city, including the former East Berlin. Herman, having only spoken German occasionally during the 38 years in America, had to engage the German side of his brain to be the translator for Judy.

Their first stop on the tour was the famous and historical Brandenburg Gate, which stands first and foremost for German reunification. On a previous short trip to Berlin, Herman and Judy visited the Brandenburg Gate of the then-divided city and looked at the armed guards of the East.

They visited many other sites in Berlin, including Potsdamer Platz, once the most bustling places in Europe. It was totally wiped out during World War II and later transformed into a death zone of the Berlin Wall. The Haenerts also visited Alexanderplatz, a large public square and transport hub of the central Middle district of Berlin near the Fernsehturm (TV Tower); and Unter den Linden, the tree-lined boulevard and former icon street of East Germany.

In East Berlin, Herman found that, sadly, nothing much had changed after years of destructive Communism. Buildings were in terrible shape, roads were crumbling, and the whole urban environment was just depressing. Throughout East Germany, people had mixed feelings: They were glad to be free of the Soviet rule, but they didn't know what to expect from fledgling capitalism.

"Old people didn't know what's going to happen to their livelihood," Herman says. "Their income had been all state-supported. At least they knew what to expect under Communism.

"It just looked like time had stood still since I left," Herman says.

When the Haenerts arrived at the Berlin Wall, still under demolition, Herman picked up a hammer and chisel and, with emotions stirring, proudly started knocking down a piece of the wall. He still has the keepsake pieces of the wall in his office as a stark reminder of the fight for freedom. Thank you, President Reagan!

The visit to Berlin included so many fascinating places, and Judy was a real trooper throughout the packed itinerary. Herman and Judy visited Charlottenburg Palace, the largest palace in Berlin; and Pergamon Museum, which houses monumental buildings such as the Pergamon Altar, the Ishtar Gate of Babylon, and many more. Although the building was severely damaged during the Second World War, many objects had been stored in safe places; significant parts of the collection remain in Russia today.

Other Berlin sites the Haenerts visited include Berliner Dom (Berlin Cathedral), a major work of Historicist architecture of the "Kaiserzeit" (Kaiser Time); Kurfurstendamm, one of the most famous avenues in Berlin and the location of the Kaiser Wilhelm Memorial Church, which was badly damaged during the war. The damaged spire of the old church has been retained as a reminder of the war.

The tour continued with Checkpoint Charlie, the name given by the Western Allies to the best-know Berlin Wall crossing point between East Berlin and West Berlin. It became the symbol of the cold war. Another stop was KaDeWe (Department Store of the West), the second-largest department store in Europe after Harrods in London. The Haenerts also saw Glienicke Bridge, which during the cold war was part of the Havel River and formed the border between West Berlin and East Germany. The bridge was used several times for the exchange of captured spies like Gary Powers, the U-2 spy plane pilot. Many movies were filmed at this bridge, which became known as the bridge of spies.

The family visited many more Berlin sites on this packed vacation, including Cecilienhof - a palace in Potsdam and meeting place on July 17th, 1945, when Harry Truman, Winston Churchill and Joseph Stalin finalized a post-World War II agreement. Herman and Judy also visited Johannesstift Spandau, where Herman lived as a boy in 1952 and 1953. He and Judy climbed the bell tower (a long way up) to find Herman's initials that he had carved into the wood during one of his bell-ringing duties. After 38 years, the marks were still visible.

While in Berlin, Herman and Judy enjoyed lots of good food and drinks in many famous Berlin restaurants with Troudchen and Hanjo. They had fun in the city, but then they moved on to a rural road trip to visit Herman's roots.

Kahlwinkel

It was time to plan the travel route to Kahlwinkel from Berlin to visit cousin Karl and other Haenert relatives. This wasn't an easy task, since it was long before GPS. They had to rely on maps that had not been updated during the Communist time in East Germany.

They rented a bright red Mercedes Benz and drove into East Germany, where people didn't have such colorful and fancy cars. They followed Hanjo and Troudchen out of Berlin, as she insisted on taking her shortcuts to get out of the city. She was a very determined Haenert, and developed this strength from her own experience hiding from the Russians.

Herman and Judy drove to Kahlwinkel over terrible roads, where his father's homestead still stood; cousin Carl and his wife, Dorchen, still lived there. Herman only got lost once - not bad, but it certainly helped that he could speak German to get directions. He still has the map that a friendly person drew for him to get out of the city and on the route to Kahlwinkel.

The family members had an emotional reunion when they saw each other for the first time in years. They spent many hours over food and drink on the first afternoon and into the late night. Herman and Judy slept in the same upstairs bedroom where Herman stayed when he was 6 years old. The house was still very primitive – there was only one downstairs bathroom, which had been somewhat modernized. It had no hot water; for shower purposes, residents had to heat the water the old-fashioned way on a stove. They still had only natural alarm clocks: roosters crowing early in the morning.

Karl and Dorchen had organized many visits to the Haenert relatives, most of them first Cousins and their families. Some visits were a total surprise, like Paula and family in Buttstädt. Paula is the daughter of Hugo and Tosca Senger, and her mother Tosca is Herman's father's sister. Paula and her husband, Kurt, owned a small retail shop of spirits. One day, Herman walked into the store and asked for Paula. The young man behind the counter asked Herman who he was; Herman identified himself as her cousin from America. The man ran upstairs to get Paula, and the family quickly organized a reunion. All the relatives of the Senger family who were close by came to see Herman and Judy from America. The party went into the late night.

The red Mercedes got a lot of exposure as the Haenerts visited many relatives, including Herman's cousin Walter Kunze, from his mother's side of the family, in Mertendorf. Every place they went, people quickly organized a party.

Herman and Judy took Karl and Dorchen on a vacation - something they had not done for a long time. One of the trip's highlights was a very steep climb to visit the Wartburg Castle - the place where Martin Luther hid and translated the New Testament from the original Greek into German. They visited a lot of Karl's and Dorchen's friends, most of whom they had not seen for a long time. Driving on the Autobahn with no speed limit was a real thrill for Herman.

The family toured a lot the former Communist checkpoints, which were filled with many miserable memories for the people who were tormented. They also visited Buchenwald, the concentration camp just outside of Weimar. It was a very disturbing and gruesome experience.

After the touring, the time came to say "Auf Wiedersehen" to Karl and Dorchen and the many memories of joyful reunions and celebrations. The Haenerts now were headed to Ramin, where he was born and grew up until the escape from communism.

Ramin

Using the sketchy maps, the Haenerts found their way to Ramin. Surprisingly, Herman remembered a lot of the roads around the Ramin vicinity.

They got an invitation to stay with their old across-the-street neighbors, Werner and Ilse Weyer. Again, it was party time, with late nights of recollections over the finest liquor they saved for special occasions. Werner and Ilse arranged a visit for Herman and Judy to tour his old home, now occupied by a very nice young couple. They were very accommodating, and seeing the home brought back a lot of memories for Herman. Herman took Judy on the escape trail - although this time in the Mercedes, not on foot like he and his Dad did in 1952.

Herman and Judy also visited Jutta Steffen, his cousin from his mother's side who lived in Ramin. Herman's mother and Jutta never got along very well, so it was kind of a strained visit. But, all ended well.

Another friend of the family, Horst and Gina Karkossa, invited Herman and Judy to stay with them for a couple of nights. Horst and Gina had escaped to West Germany and since the wall came down, they were able to reclaim their family's property in Ramin. Horst and Gina arranged a tour of the church where Herman's family worshipped, the school that Herman attended, and a reunion with one of Herman's old classmates. Again, they had lots of good food, drinks, laughter, remembrances, and late nights.

Everyplace Herman and Judy went, meeting family and friends of Herman's family, Judy was awesome. Despite the difficulty of not being able communicate in German and depending completely on Herman's translations, her smile and gestures communicated her feelings and responses to any conversation.

Time had gone by fast, and it was time to leave Ramin and drive back to Berlin to return that red Mercedes and fly back to Chicago. The Haenerts left their refreshing experience in Europe filled with many memories and an appreciation of our great country. They were proud to be Americans, and Herman had no desire to return to Germany. And soon, on the other side of the Atlantic, their new life in Arizona would begin.

After returning home to America, Herman and Judy would return to Germany two more times: in 2002 with their daughter Heidi, son-in-law David and grandchildren Dillon and Ben; and in 2014 with their son, Jay. A reporter for the German publication Nordkurier wrote an article about Herman and his family during the most recent visit.

Den alten Ami kennen wir doch: Klar, das ist Herman
We know this old American: Without question, it is Herman

Wiedersehen in Ramin: Hier wurde Herman Haenert (2. v. l.) geboren. Heute lebt der 73-Jährige mit seiner Frau Judith (Mitte) und Sohn Hans (52) in Tucson im US-Bundesstaat Arizona. Gina Karkossa (links) kannte die Eltern von Herman Heanert, Erich und Toska, gut. Rechts Barbara Rach, die mit ihrem Mann Roland im Geburtshaus von Herman Haenert

Reunion in Ramin: Here is where Herman Haenert was born. Today the 73 year old lives with his wife Judith (in the middle) and son Hans (52) in Tucson, Arizona. Gina Karkossa (on the left) knew Herman Haenert's parents Erich and Tosca very well. On the right is Barbara Rach, who with her husband Roland live in the house where Herman was born.

wohnt. FOTO: f. lucius
VonFred Lucius

Das ist schon
eine spannende Familiengeschichte:
Familie Haenert aus Ramin wanderte nach Amerika aus, kehrte nach Deutschland zurück und wanderte
wieder aus. Herman Haenert besuchte jetzt mit seiner Familie seinen Geburtsort – und staunte, wie schön
es hier ist.

This is really an exciting family story:

The Haenert Family from Ramin immigrated to America, returned to Germany and immigrated again to America. Herman Haenert and his family visited his place of birth and commented how nice it looked.

Ramin.Zwölf Jahre liegt der letzte Besuch von Herman Haenert zurück. „Es hat sich viel verändert. Die Wege sind besser", meint der 73-Jährige und zeigt auf den Schmagerower Weg in Ramin. Dort, im

Haus Nummer 16, wurde er geboren. „Es ist aber das zweite Haus an dieser Stelle.

Ramin. It has been twelve years since Herman Haenert's last visit to Ramin. Much has changed. The streets have improved said the 73 year old and pointed to the (Schmagerower Weg) (the name of the street in front of the house). There, in house number 16 is where he was born. However, this is the 2nd house on this plot of ground

Das erste haben die Russen 1945 abgebrannt", erzählt Herman Haenert, der heute mit seiner Frau Judith (72) in Tucson im US-Bundesstaat Arizona lebt. Das ist auch die Heimat von Sohn Hans (52). Die Heimat der Eltern Erich und Toska, den Geburtsort von Herman, die wollen sich die drei Haenerts ansehen.

Die Geschichte der aus Ramin stammenden Familie ist ungewöhnlich. 1923 wanderten Erich und Toska nach Amerika aus.

The Russians burnt down the first house in 1945, said Herman Haenert, who today with his Judith (72) live in Tucson, AZ. That also is the home of their Son Hans (52). The birthplace of his parents Erich and Tosca, the birthplace of Herman are on the trip agenda of the three Haenerts. The story of the family originating from Ramin is unusual. In 1923 Erich and Tosca immigrated to America.

Zehn Jahre später, 1933, kehrten sie zurück. Das Gut Ramin wurde in jenem Jahr aufgesiedelt, auch die Haenerts erhielten Platz für Haus und Hof. „Zum Kriegsende sind alle Raminer vor den Russen geflüchtet. Wir wollten zu den Amerikanern, sind Richtung Berlin", erinnert sich Herman Haenert, damals fünf Jahre alt. Wahrscheinlich, weil ein Tresor im Haus stand, ist es abgefackelt worden, vermutet er. Wiederaufbau nach dem Krieg. Anfang der 50er-Jahre ließ die Familie schließlich erneut alles hinter sich und kehrte Ramin wieder den Rücken. „Mein Vater hat gesagt, wir müssen hier raus", blickt der

73-Jährige zurück. Land und Vieh mussten in der LPG eingebracht
werden. Das wollte der Vater nicht.

Ten years later, in 1933 they came back to Germany and settled in
Ramin because of land opportunities during that time, to have a
home and land for farming. As the war was coming to an end, the
entire population of Ramin packed up and left to run away from
the anticiapation of the Russians coming into Ramin. We were all
trying to meet the American Army, and traveled in the direction
of Berlin, remembered Herman Haenert, five years old at the time.
Because we had a safe in our house, the Russians torched the house,
is his supposition. We build a new house after the war.

In the beginning of the 1950's the decision was made to leave everything new behind, and turned the back on Ramin. My Father
said " we need to get out of here", as the 73 year old looked back.
Land and livestock had to be under the control of the LPG (the
communist). My father did not want that at all.

In einer Nacht- und Nebel-Aktion, ohne dass die Nachbarn etwas
merkten, ging es nach Westberlin. „Das mit dem Auswandern war gar
nicht so einfach", schildert Herman Haenert.

During one foggy night the mission to leave was undertaken, without the neighbors awareness, we made our way to Westberlin. But
not everything was easy.

Weil seine Papiere nicht vollständig waren, konnte er nicht mit den
Eltern mit, die 1952 nach Amerika übersiedelten. Ein Jahr lang war das
christliche Johannesstift in Berlin die Adresse von Herman Haenert.
Dann konnte auch er über den großen Teich.

Because of a propblem with his immigration papers, he could not
immigrate to America with his parents in 1952 and lived in a

Christian Johannesstift in Berlin for one year. Following the year in Berlin, he was able to cross the big pond.

Dort betrieb er ein Geschäft für Tierarzt-Artikel.

Erneut und dauerhaft nach Ramin zurückkehren, dass will der 73-Jährige nicht. Aber immer wieder zu Besuch kommen in die alte Heimat und in den Geburtsort. Auch seinem Enkel Zachary (29) will er das noch zeigen. „Du kannst noch so viel erzählen und Bilder zeigen. Das reicht nicht. Du musst es sehen", meint Herman Haenert.

There he is involved in a veterinary –animal health business.

The 73 year old has no plans to return to Ramin on a permanent basis, but to visit the old home country and my place of birth is still on the agenda. My Grandson Zachary (29) has to see it. You can talk a lot and look at pictures, that's not enough, you must see it" said Herman Haenert

Chapter 13

Tucson

Moving from Illinois to Arizona involves a dramatic change, but it was a long time coming. Judy's parents had been spending winters in Tucson, and she and Herman enjoyed visiting there. The Haenerts discussed purchasing a retirement home in sunny Arizona or Florida – and, as they spent more time in Tucson, they grew more and more fond of the desert and decided to buy property there.

In 1990, Herman and Judy decided to build a retirement home in Arizona and split their time 50-50 between the chilly Midwest and the warm desert. First, they spent four days in the Phoenix area looking at properties - but Phoenix was too busy and had too much traffic, so they chose the more mellow Tucson.

On previous visits to Tucson, they had looked at numerous retirement communities including one called Saddlebrooke, meant for residents 55 and older. Although the community was 14 miles from the closest grocery store and other services, the Haenerts took another look at Saddlebrooke. They were under 55, but the community allowed 15 percent of homeowners to be under the age floor.

Once the Haenerts made the turn onto the neighborhood's Saddlebrooke Boulevard, they spotted the beautiful mountain view and made up their minds: This is the place for us. The couple quickly purchased an empty lot on the golf course; it had a beautiful view. Although they were not required to build a house within a certain time frame, Herman and Judy built their Arizona home there in 1991.

Living in Tucson, A.K.A. "The Old Pueblo"

At first, the Haenerts thought this new home would be a second home – a place where they would spend up to half of their time, and where they would move some time in the future. But they loved the new place, and longed to live there full-time sooner rather than later.

Herman and Judy's family knew about their desire to have a place in a warm part of the country, but they did not know that they'd decided to make the move to Tucson permanent. Then, during a golf game with their daughter Heidi and son-in-law David at Forest Hills Country Club, the younger couple announced that they had news for them: "You are going to be Grandpa and Grandma!" Following that excitement, Herman and Judy replied: "We have news for you also. We are moving to Tucson permanently!"

Herman gave ConAgra a full year's notice that he would be leaving, so that the company could have plenty of time to find his replacement. Although ConAgra offered Herman the opportunity to continue to run the ConAgra animal-health business from Tucson, he decided to pursue an opportunity offered to him by AgriLabs. The timing and the professional opportunity were perfect: AgriLabs needed representation in the west to work with the AgriLabs distributors to grow their businesses, and they needed an experienced business-development person.

Herman and Scott Remington, AgriLabs president, had worked closely together for a number of years, and came to an employment agreement.

They presented the job offer to the AgriLabs Board for approval, and the members accepted it. Herman's AgriLabs career was ready to be launched as part of the team.

So, the Haenerts made their final move from Rockford to Tucson in September of 1992. Then, in October, Herman started his new job with AgriLabs.

AgriLabs - Beginnings

Herman was passionate about making AgriLabs a success, since he had founded it, served on its board of directors, and was part owner of the real estate. Ever since the inception of AgriLabs in 1984, Herman had supported the company with a huge focus on its product line as part of Wholesale Vet. With his background of building a business and his "big corporate, public company experience" with ConAgra, Herman was very ready to help AgriLabs members with their strategies.

Plan in hand, Herman started his new career at AgriLabs with a great lineup of talent. Scott Remington was president, Denny Feary was sales/marketing manager, and Terry Christie was head of R&D. Other key colleagues included David Zehender, Sam Gentry, and Kerr Broadstreet.

One of Herman's former employees - Dennis "Denny" Feary, who was a representative for Herman in Northern Illinois, Eastern Iowa and Southern Wisconsin – also joined the AgriLabs team. Denny and Scott Remington had become good friends, because Scott worked with Denny in the field as part of his job as AgriLabs president. Although Herman was not very happy that Scott had hired Denny to become Midwest regional manager, they agreed that it was a growth opportunity for Denny.

Prior to joining AgriLabs, Herman, Scott Remington, and three other board members had negotiated to purchase the 49 percent of the Fermentia-owned shares via acquisition of TechAmerica. It was a long and tedious pursuit to get the best deal for the AgriLabs shareholders, but the businessmen were able to negotiate a fair deal. This deal resulted in 100 percent ownership for the shareholders, all intellectual property in question, and a supply agreement.

Scott and Herman met to outline the goals and expected outcomes for Herman's contribution to the AgriLabs team. They had a long to-do list of things they wanted to accomplish, starting with planning sessions with each AgriLabs member in the West, setting goals, and implementing plans to achieve them. The team met with other AgriLabs members who asked to work with Herman, to take advantage of his knowledge and experience. The leaders searched for opportunities to use the aggregate AgriLabs' purchasing power to reduce costs and increase profits.

Then, the team sought product acquisitions, product development, and product licensing opportunities. They began international marketing of AgriLabs products, and added additional AgriLabs members.

AgriLabs – Growth

Herman was off to a running start, working primarily with AgriLabs distributors in Hanford and City of Industry, California; and Seattle and Yakima, Washington; WA. He also worked with JR Simplot Western Stockmen's in Caldwell, Idaho. Along with Herman's close and continued working relationships with the AgriLabs distributors, he started exploring the combined purchasing power of the AgriLabs distributors with other new product/business ventures. Herman explored many areas including health insurance, general insurance, freight rates, UPS /Airborne contracts, credit cards, long distance telephone rate opportunities, and fleet leasing /purchasing of trucks and automobiles.

Herman started working with AT&T in the Kansas Region to explore a deal that would drastically reduce the long-distance cost for all AgriLabs members, in the age before cell phones. He compiled one year's data of every member's long-distance usage and submitted the data to AT&T, which was interested in striking a deal for a new program called Uniplan. AgriLabs would enter into a three-year contract with AT&T on behalf of its members/distributors, and have separate billing for each distributor. Herman negotiated a rate that saved each member/distributor 33 percent, and AgriLabs received a $125,000 upfront payment. It was a win-win for everyone, and the company renewed for another three-year period with similar terms.

Herman negotiated a National Account status for AgriLabs with Airborne and UPS, resulting in significant savings for the AgriLabs team: 15 percent on ground rates, 50 percent on Next Day Air, and 35 percent on 2nd day air. It was a great deal for the AgriLabs team!

He also negotiated a fleet incentive program with PHH Fleet America to allow AgriLabs and its members to get economical leasing for trucks, cars and forklifts, previously only available to large corporations. Through the contract, members also could purchase vehicles through the fleet-pricing structure of Ford, GM, Chrysler, Toyota, GMC, and other manufacturers.

Herman also had negotiated an insurance package, but the members were hesitant to change from their current carriers because of pre-existing conditions and local agent representation.

All of his efforts led to growth for AgriLabs and its distributors, with innovative marketing to create demand and new product introductions. Under the leadership of Terry Christie, AgriLabs was the first animal-health company to receive an FDA approval for an abbreviated new animal drug (ANADA) called Di-Methox, a broad-spectrum antibiotic approved for dairy cattle, beef cattle, calves, turkeys and chickens. An ANADA approval clears the way for generic drugs, after the pioneer products expire. It takes capital and knowledgeable people like Terry Christie to get the job done.

The FDA's approval of Di-Methox for the animal-health industry really put AgriLabs on the map. The company continued its investments into the filing of ANADAs, and the business now own 13 approvals.

This exciting new AgriLabs phase in Herman's career encompassed his daily life, and he often left his Tucson home for business trips. Meeting with the AgriLabs members and owners became a family affair, as some of them invited Herman to stay at their homes rather than rent a hotel room. The Tucson airport - and especially, the personnel at America West Airlines - became very well acquainted with Herman, as he traveled extensively during his 13 years at AgriLabs.

Herman hit a major bump in the road in the mid-'90s, as he was diagnosed with bladder cancer. It required two surgeries and two rounds of treatments with BCG, which is a drug used for treatment of tuberculosis. As of 2018, Herman has been cancer-free for 24 years. Despite his illness, he kept traveling and pursuing more opportunities for AgriLabs.

Besides the cancer, though, another crisis came up during the '90s, when Herman lost a lot of his savings from a deal that went bad.

Subpoena from the United States Security and Exchange Commission, Dated January 26th, 1996

Herman had invested in securities and start-up companies that had great potential in new and emerging technologies, and one of those companies was called Work Recovery, Inc. A broker friend name Patrick Lambert introduced him to the company, and he presented Herman with an investment opportunity in very interesting technology.

WRI's main product was the ERGOS system, a multi-phased device used to provide objective, functional capacity testing of an individual's performance of specific physical tasks. This objective evaluation can measure the extent of a worker's disability, determine the worker's qualifications for returning to work or alternative employment, and develop and monitor physical-therapy programs. The system was marketed directly to healthcare providers, insurers, and large employers at a price of $125,000.

Ironically, WRI was based in Tucson, which gave Herman the opportunity to visit the company's headquarters on a regular basis. He became very good friends with Tom Brandon, WRI's president and co-founder.

Herman kept investing in the company, including with margin purchases, based on published reports of growth and demand for the product. The Social Security Administration had requested a demonstration to help verify disability claims, and this elevated the share price to $8. Herman's portfolio value of WRI shares exceeded over $1,000,000. It was time to sell, but Herman thought about all the taxes to be paid, and he was enticed by the experts' projection of a $15 stock. (The lesson: Don't be a pig.)

In a 1995 Wall Street Journal article, John Emshwiller reported that Brandon had conducted allegedly shady financial deals that federal agencies were investigating; the feds were uncovering false filings to the Securities and Exchange Commission. Brandon was charged with eight criminal counts, including mail fraud, security fraud, and falsifying company records.

The day the article was published, panic selling set in, the shares dropped to $3.00, and margin calls, including to Herman, hit the street. A portion of Herman's equities evaporated to meet the margin call. That was last time Herman ever purchased stocks on borrowed money.

The SEC investigated Tom Brandon and large shareholders, including Herman. It was not a fun time being drilled by four SEC attorneys at the federal court house in Tucson, and producing volumes of documents.

The SEC did not care about gains or losses - only if Herman had any inside information, which he did not. The SEC found no improprieties in Herman's buying and selling of WRI shares. Herman's friends familiar with his large losses in the WRI stock encouraged and comforted him by the words that still ring in his ears today: "You will make it back, plus."

As the saying goes, not all that glitters is gold.

Chapter **14**

AgriLabs, AgriLabs and More AgriLabs

The AgriLabs years of Herman's life were so productive and multifaceted that it warrants a whole new chapter with more details just about AgriLabs.

Herman negotiated volume rebate contracts with numerous companies including the Andover Company (co-flex bandages), Ideal Instrument Company (veterinary syringes and needles, etc.) All these agreements contributed to the profitability of AgriLabs and its members/owners.

During Herman's tenure, the AgriLabs business was growing in volume and profitability. Under his leadership, the ProLabs line grew substantially, as more members established relationships with veterinarians either as employees or consultants. Most of the ProLabs products required prescriptions from a veterinarian in order to have downline sales to the end user.

The mid-1990s saw some major management changes at AgriLabs, as Scott Remington resigned as company president. One of the board

108

members called Herman, informed him of Scott's resignation, and asked if Herman would be interested in the position – but he declined, as the position would require a move to St. Joseph, Missouri. Herman declined and offered to help in any way he could on a temporary basis; and, he recommended Denny Feary for the position.

Denny became President of AgriLabs following Scott Remington's resignation. Herman traveled to St. Joseph for many weeks to assist the new president with numerous projects and management challenges. Denny insisted that Herman stay at his house and save the hotel costs.

Now that Denny had become president, AgriLabs soon had to hire a replacement for his former sales and marketing position. Fortunately, a number of great potential candidates were becoming available because of animal-health consolidation. That was the case with Steve Schram, a former Syntex Animal Health employee. Herman and Denny knew Steve very well from the Wholesale Vet days, as Rockford-base Steve was a territory manager for Syntex and worked closely with all Wholesale Veterinary Supply field representatives and management personnel.

Steve accepted the position of Sales and Marketing Manager. His experience and management background made AgriLabs and Steve the perfect match. His creative-marketing plans, staffing, and leadership of the sales force were very successful.

Steve hired a young, energetic and visionary person by the name of Vince Palasota for the southwest regional manager position. Herman, Denny and Steve interviewed Vince until the wee morning hours at St. Joseph's finest - a very memorable night for Herman. Vince got the job and became AgriLabs vice president of sales, but he didn't stay that long. Vince's entrepreneurial skills and drive consummated in his resignation from AgriLabs and the start of his own business ventures. Vince is highly successful and still enjoying the fruits of his labors today. He is a great family man and a very special friend of Herman's.

AgriLabs Loses its President

Denny thoughtfully constructed AgriLabs' short-term/long-term plans where thoughtfully, and he set the course for long term growth and survivability. Tragically, Denny's era came to an end on January 28th, 1997.

On that fateful night, Herman was on a late-night flight to Kansas City to attend the National Cattlemen's meeting. David Zehender met Herman at the airport during the late hour, to Herman's surprise; he suspected something was definitely wrong. Without any greetings, David broke the news: "Denny died tonight."

Herman was in total shock, and the entire AgriLabs family was in disbelief. At the age of 43, Denny had suffered a major heart attack and died at the hospital in St. Joseph, Missouri. On February 1st, 1997, Denny was buried in Oregon, Illinois. Aside from the AgriLabs family, many industry people paid their respects to Denny on a very cold and blustery day.

The AgriLabs board members and others stayed overnight at a Chicago O'Hare Airport hotel. With no disrespect for Denny, the board met after the funeral at the O'Hare Hilton and offered the job of AgriLabs president to Steve Schram, who accepted the challenge.

Herman's duties changed following Denny's death, as Steve asked Herman to devote all of his time to business development. Herman already had numerous projects in the beginning stages of development, and his time was more valuable to focus on new growth opportunities.

Relationships are so important in life and business - and that is why Herman pursued a major opportunity for AgriLabs with Diamond Laboratories in Des Moines, Iowa. He met with a friend – a new employee of Diamond Laboratories in Las Vegas - during the Western Veterinary Conference. This friend gave Herman a detailed overview of a new line of cattle vaccines in development by Diamond Laboratories. Confidential negotiations started in Tucson, Arizona with Herman; Lou Van Daele, president of Diamond Laboratories; and their chief scientific officer, Mike McGinley. The new technology, once approved by the USDA, would be the first of its kind in the cattle-vaccine marketing place.

Months of negotiations followed, and they were challenging: How can a relatively small AgriLabs compete in licensing this breakthrough technology against the big pharma companies?

Despite many obstacles, AgriLabs put out a press release of June 24th, 1998 that said this: "Agri Laboratories, Ltd. announced that they have been awarded exclusive worldwide marketing rights to a new line of livestock vaccines (Titanium and Masterguard) being developed by Des Moines-based Diamond Animal Health, a division of Heska Corporation."

It was a great day for AgriLabs and Herman.

Norbrook and Ireland

AgriLabs' brand names of Titanium and Masterguard became highly effective and widely used cattle vaccines that are the icon of AgriLabs. It's funny how things turn out: Big pharma Elanco, a division of Eli Lilly, purchased Titanium and Masterguard from AgriLabs in 2013.

During his AgriLabs career, Herman negotiated many deals with many companies, including: The Neogen Corporation, Grand Laboratories, Intervet, Bayer, Schering, Biocor, Virbac, Anthony Products, Norbrook, Farnam, Immtech, Sergeant's Pet Care, Animal Health Ventures, Andover Company, and Carter Wallace, to name a few.

Each one of the deals has its own experiences and memories, but the Norbrook deal is especially memorable for Herman. This company is located in Ireland and owned by then-Senator Dr. Ed Haughey (later Baron Ballyedmond, member of the House of Lords).

Ironically, Herman competed with Dr. Ed Haughey to acquire the assets of the Maury Company in California during Herman's ConAgra days. The key assets of the Norbrook were two FDA-approved penicillin products. Dr. Haughey outbid Herman and moved the products to his manufacturing facility in Ireland, in anticipation of marketing the products in the U.S. as soon as the FDA gave its approval. Dr. Haughey and Herman stayed in contact during that time.

Dr. Haughey called Herman and said: "I am sending my administrative assistant, Ann Murney, to Tucson to meet with you and design a basic plan for AgriLabs and Norbrooke to work together." Ann did meet with Herman in Tucson, and they negotiated a preliminary plan; however, as time went on, the parties could not agree on certain deal points. Herman received a call from Dr. Haughey and he said: "I am sending you a first-class ticket to fly to my office in Ireland. Here is a list of dates, so pick one. I want a face-to-face meeting."

Herman accepted his offer to meet, and flew across the Atlantic to meet with Dr. Haughey and his team at their office in Newry, a city located in Northern Ireland. During the two days of meetings, Norbrook and AgriLabs decided on a distribution agreement, and made a handshake deal to work together on future products that were in Norbrook's pipeline.

Dr. Haughey invited Herman to join him and his wife, Mary, for dinner at his castle. Dr. Haughey's chauffer picked Herman up from his hotel and dropped him off at the castle. Herman asked the chauffer what time he was going to pick up after dinner, and the chauffer replied: "If Dr. Haughey likes you, it could be 1 a.m.; if he does not like you, it will 10 p.m." Herman must have made a great impression, because he left the castle at 1:30 a.m.

As Herman arrived at the castle, the butler met him and announced his arrival to Dr. and Mrs. Haughey. The castle had been completely redone and looked absolutely stunning, like a movie set. Following introductions, Dr. Haughey invited Herman to have drinks outside of the castle overlooking the Irish Sea. The host detailed his business philosophies and the resulting successes in the global animal-health businesses: Dr. Haughey had built numerous veterinary pharmaceutical manufacturing facilities, funded by the Northern Ireland government and private investors.

Martin Murdock, Dr. Haughey's chief financial officer, joined them for dinner, and made it an even better and more memorable evening. Herman and Dr. Haughey became good friends.

The relationship between AgriLabs and Norbrook prospered, and the companies are still doing business together today. After the first Ireland visit, Dr. Haughey invited Herman, Steve Schram, and Terry Christie to fly first-class back to the Emerald Isle to explore mutual opportunities.

Sadly, Dr. Haughey, like Denny Feary, met an untimely end. He, his pilot and co-pilot were killed in a tragic helicopter crash on March 13th, 2014. He died the second richest man in Northern Ireland. Ironically, Steve Schram recently had resigned his position of AgriLabs president, and became the head of Norbrook, North America.

Herman was always reminded that in order to be successful, one must accept failures and move on, knowing that failure is a natural consequence of trying. He had experienced several of his own failures during his career, including attempts to negotiate other two other vaccine opportunities. These deals fell through, mostly because of unforeseen regulatory issues and additional capital requirements.

Sometimes, one has to pull the plug and move on, and learn from the experience. If you're not big enough to lose, you're not big enough to win.

The Merck Agreement

As mentioned previously, each deal during Herman's 13-year active career at AgriLabs has its own memorable achievements and failures. Aside from the great success of Titanium and Masterguard cattle vaccines, two other major agreements immensely contributed to AgriLabs market position and growth.

As with many of Herman's thoughts and ideas, he always discussed them with the president of AgriLabs: Scott Remington, Denny Feary and Steve Schram, now all former presidents. They were always very open-minded, no matter how crazy the ideas seemed at the time. This was the case with an idea Herman presented to Denny in 1995 regarding a key animal-health product, Ivomec, owned and marketed by a major pharmaceutical company called Merck/Merial.

The compound, Ivermectin, was coming off of its patent in 1997, meaning that any company that has the knowledge and a source of an approved raw-material supplier could submit an application to the FDA for an Abbreviated New Animal Drug Application (ANADA). Herman's idea was to contact an old friend - Carrol Mills, sales manager for Merck Animal Health - and discuss the possibility of a collaborative agreement between the two companies to establish another brand of Ivermectin Pour On and Injectable.

Herman did contact Carrol and arranged a meeting with Merck at the New Jersey headquarters to discuss Herman's idea. Carrol and Herman acknowledged that long-standing relationships are of immense value, and they got a meeting with the Merck Animal Health management team.

Receiving positive feedback, Herman started negotiations with Merck to establish another branded product, which would be manufactured by Merck and marketed by AgriLabs under the AgriLabs brand names of Topline Pour On and Double Impact Injectable Ivermectin. Herman believes if you wait for chances, they never come. Success can only come if you have taken chances.

Following months of intense negotiations, Merck and AgriLabs announced their collaborative agreement. It sent shock waves throughout the animal-health industry. People wondered how a relatively small animal-health company like AgriLabs can negotiate an agreement with a major global animal-health company like Merck and their leading compound, Ivermectin.

Double Impact and Top Line Pour On became AgriLabs' leading products for a number of years, and really put AgriLabs on the map as a major animal-health company.

The Epitopix Agreement

Bill Barr, AgriLabs sales manager in 2003, dropped Herman a note and asked him to follow up on a visit he had with a company called Epitopix, a subsidiary of Minnesota-based Willmar Poultry Co. Bill informed Herman that Epitopix was developing a new vaccine that could be of interest to AgriLabs.

Herman made contact with the company and started a dialogue with Dr. Jim Sandstrom, sales and sarketing manager for Epitopix. Dr. Sandstrom informed Herman that Willmar Poultry Co. had formed a company called Epitopix, and hired knowledgeable research personnel to develop a salmonella vaccine; this would control a major disease in poultry and other species. AgriLabs had interest in controlling salmonella in cattle.

Following the execution of a non-disclosure agreement, Jim Sandstrom and Epitopix disclosed their technology to AgriLabs, including the work that had been done on cattle. Herman and the AgriLabs team evaluated the technology and determined that there would be a great demand for the Epitopix futuristic and broad-spectrum salmonella product for cattle.

Herman expressed the AgriLabs interest to Dr. Sandstrom, and they arranged a meeting at the Willmar Poultry/ Epitopix headquarters in Willmar, Minnesota. Herman and Steve Schram met with the Epitopix team on April 17, 2003; participants included Ted Huisinga, president of Willmar Poultry Company, Inc.

Herman and Steve presented the AgriLabs capabilities and their interest in the technology. The Epitopix team presented a broad overview, and an in-depth, up-to-date research and development report.

Both parties agreed they had a common interest and to continue to communicate; they agreed to meet in the future as needed to make a deal. Ted Huisinga, a very smart and skillful negotiator, kept reminding Herman that AgriLabs was not the only potential partner: He was working with big pharma and their deep pockets, and was less risk than AgriLabs. This is not the first time that Herman had to overcome those obstacles, and he used prior successes as a base for continuing negotiations.

Numerous meetings followed the April 17 meeting. Herman had negotiated the AgriLabs position to the point that Ted Huisinga agreed to a meeting at the Minneapolis Airport Northwest Airlines Club. Herman and Steve Schram knew this was the win-or-lose meeting as they prepared for that day. Following an exhaustive and intense final negotiating session, Ted agreed that it would be in the best interest to enter into a marketing relationship with AgriLabs, rather than big pharma.

It was another great day for AgriLabs. To this day, Ted Huisinga refers to Herman as the "Silver Fox." It turned out be a great business deal for both parties, and AgriLabs and Epitopix are still doing business as of this date.

New Members

Recruiting independent animal health companies to become part of the AgriLabs family was challenging. Any new member company would have to purchase stock in AgriLabs based on the current share value, which had appreciated substantially since its inception. AgriLabs would have to present a financial payback formula for any new owner.

Herman and the AgriLabs team identified numerous potential companies. The first company he contacted was Valley Vet Supply, located in Marysville, Kansas.

Then, Herman spoke to Dr. Arnold Nagley of Valley Vet Supply. This opened the door for Dr. Nagley and Dr. Schultz to come to St. Joseph, Missouri, to meet the AgriLabs team, facilities and discuss the value of joining the AgriLabs family. Dr. Nagley and Dr. Schultz astutely evaluated the opportunity, and made the investment in AgriLabs.

Dr. Nagley became very active in the AgriLabs organization, was elected to the board of directors and served in advisory capacities. Herman and Dr. Nagley became good friends.

And then came VetPharm Inc., based in Sioux Falls, South Dakota. Herman had established a relationship with Chuck Vander Ploeg, the company president. The two met during an AVDA meeting in Colorado Springs, Colorado. Herman presented the AgriLabs story to Chuck, hoping a beneficial relationship might be established. Since VetPharm sold only to veterinarians, Herman advised Chuck that they would be a great addition to the AgriLabs family – and, joining would be an outstanding opportunity for VetPharm.

Herman arranged a meeting in St. Joseph, Missouri to meet the AgriLabs team, tour the facilities, and get an in-depth overview of AgriLabs capabilities. Chuck Vander Ploeg and Brent Van Der Swaag represented VetPharm at the meeting, and then a dinner at St. Joe Country Club. The memorable part of the evening was Herman getting lost going to the country club because of road construction in the area. Chuck and Brent still remember that part of the evening today. What an impression he made!

VetPharm made the investment to become part of the AgriLabs family of companies, thankfully. Chuck became active in the organization and served on the AgriLabs Board of Directors.

AVDA meetings always present a great platform for all industry people to get acquainted, form friendships and explore mutual opportunities. Herman was paired with Jim Cleary, who had recently become president of MWI Veterinary Supply, at the annual AVDA golf outing. While the two men shared a golf cart, Herman talked to Jim about a possible membership/ownership in AgriLabs. Jim said his company already had a membership in a competitive organization (VEDCO), but he was open to exploring the possibility.

Jim invited Herman to come to MWI's Idaho headquarters and meet with the MWI management team. The team was impressed with Herman's presentation, and it established a baseline for additional meetings between the management of both companies. Both companies found ways to overcome numerous obstacles, and MWI made the investment and became a major contributor to the AgriLabs growth-management team.

The team was impressed with Herman's presentation and established a baseline for additional meetings between the management of both companies. Both companies found ways to overcome numerous obstacles and MWI made the investment and became a major contributor to AgriLabs growth management team. The team was impressed with Herman's presentation and established a baseline for additional meetings between the management of both companies. Both companies found ways to overcome numerous obstacles and MWI made the investment and became a major contributor to AgriLabs growth.

China

China, a country of 1.2 billion people, had to explore all possibilities to feed its people. Although a Communist Country, their economy, ironically, is driven by the engine of capitalism. The Chinese livestock industry was not well organized, until Western technologies and agricultural consultants from the U.S. and other countries helped to established large dairy, swine and poultry operations instead of a scattered livestock industry of small operators.

U.S. animal-health companies started to invest capital with Chinese partners to take advantage of the underserved opportunities in the Chinese animal-health market. A Dr. Mark Xiao, who represented a Chinese company in that industry, contacted Herman to express interest in AgriLabs' Titanium and Masterguard vaccine lines. Herman and the AgriLabs management team had numerous meetings with Dr. Xiao to explore all opportunities available to AgriLabs in China, including an investment in a new biological and pharmaceutical plant in Chengdu, China.

Herman and Terry Christie, vice president of research and development, flew to China in April of 2004 to meet with the Chinese delegation of potential Chinese animal-health partners, including Yuanheng Pharmaceuticals Co. The Chinese rolled out the red carpet everywhere Herman and Terry had meetings. The Chinese delegations consisted of former high-level government employees, investment bankers, former Chinese FDA officials, and representatives of pharmaceutical manufacturers and distributors.

High-level meetings took place in the office of the Chengdu mayor, site visits to animal health pharmaceutical companies, and potential building sites in a new industrial development. The Chinese company also hired the services of Michael Dobbs Higginson, formerly head of Merrill Lynch Asia as their investment advisor. Michael was the person that insisted on a meeting in China and was the lead person along with Dr. Xiao in all the meetings.

At the conclusion of all the meetings, toasts and explorations, the Chinese delegation and Michael Dobbs Higginson insisted on a signed Memorandum Of Understanding (MOU). That was a difficult task considering the time difference between China and the AgriLabs attorney in Kansas City, Missouri – and available translation services.

Terry and Herman left China with a better understanding of the opportunities for AgriLabs, the risk assessment, and the sharing of intellectual property (IP). The Chinese delegation, including Michael Dobbs Higginson, met in St. Joseph for a follow up meeting.

Yet, after peeling back all layers of the onion, AgriLabs passed on the opportunity in China, for good reasons and the advice of Michael Dobbs Higginson, who became a good friend of Herman's

The Chinese have a very clever way of interlocking many companies. At the end, it is difficult to figure out with whom you are doing business and in what country they are incorporated.

Nonetheless, the China chapter was a great learning experience for Herman, Terry, and the AgriLabs team.

Retirement and Scholarship

Herman retired from AgriLabs as a full-time employee in 2005. Steve Schram arranged a retirement event for Herman with most of the AgriLabs members/owners in attendance.

Herman really made his mark on the company. The *AgriLabs/Herman Haenert Scholarship Fund was established in 2005 to honor and recognize the contributions that Herman made to AgriLabs while serving as vice president of business development from 1992 to 2005.*

One $5,000 scholarship is available to employees and immediate family members of AgriLabs and its shareholders who are in pursuit of a two- or a four-year college degree in any field of study. A GPA of 2.5 and above must be maintained with a minimum of 12 credit hours per semester. A current transcript must be included with the application.

Chapter *15*

Net Vet Supply, Etc.

Herman "retired" as a full-time employee of AgriLabs in 2005, and he formed a consulting company called Net Vet Supply, LLC. Net Vet Supply also offered a platform to sell short-dated and discontinued animal-health products. The website (platform) had a design similar to eBay, and the drop-ship feature on the site was similar to Amazon in the 2018 world.

Under the terms of Herman's consulting agreement with AgriLabs, he was obligated to grant the right of first refusal on any opportunity he initiated. If AgriLabs passed on the opportunity, Herman was under no obligation to AgriLabs, and retained the right to work with anyone to license and sell his initiatives and technologies. Following are some of the key initiatives that Herman pursued on his own in accordance with the terms of his agreement with AgriLabs.

During the term of this specific consulting agreement, Herman worked very closely with Steve Schram, President of AgriLabs. He negotiated numerous agreements, and offered advice to Steve and AgriLabs whenever or wherever requested.

At the time Herman started his consulting business, he had 35 years of experience in the animal-health industry, made a lot of friends, and had many contacts throughout the global animal-health scene.

ANOxA Corporation:

Herman received a call from one of those contacts, asking him to look at a development opportunity in the equine (horse) industry. The technology was in the infant stages of development. Dr. Bryan Perry and Mike Piotrowski were the principal partners in a company called Anoxa Corporation, which contacted Herman.

Without getting too technical, the technology they were looking to develop and file for FDA approval is a Type 5 inhibitor. It is similar to Viagra, only their technology is lung-related, specifically reducing the pressure in the lungs of the horses and preventing performance horses from bleeding during heavily stressed racing or exercising. This is a common and untreated ailment in horses known as exercise-induced pulmonary hemorrhaging (EIPH).

Bryan and Mike asked Herman for his advice, and agreed to a meeting in Las Vegas during the Western Veterinary Conference to explore the opportunity. They shared the complete background on the technology, and how it would change the landscape of treating horses with EIPH.

In conjunction with a previously engaged partner, Dr. Perry, a pulmonary specialist, performed preliminary efficacy trials on thoroughbreds at the Macau China Racetrack. The results were presented to Herman as convincing, although the two-step inoculation was cumbersome and troubling to Herman.

Herman was intrigued by the technology, and was offered an ownership position in ANOxA Corporation and the president's title. In exchange, Herman would lead the way to raise the capital to develop and obtain FDA approval, and license or sell the technology to an animal-health company.

Herman accepted the offer. Following years of trials and tribulations, Herman was successful in negotiating a sale of the patented technology to a major pharmaceutical company. The final global sales estimates of this technology could reach $100 million annually, once approved by all the regulatory agencies. Due to confidential language in the agreement, Herman cannot disclose any details of the sale; however, it was a major payoff for all the efforts that Bryan Perry, Mike Piotrowski, and Herman contributed to the project.

Herman, Bryan and Mike retained certain rights to apply the technology in dogs and cats. They formed a new company namely VETNOx, LLC, and completed successful clinical studies to treat pulmonary hypertension in dogs. At this time, VETNOx is considering the best strategy to introduce the technology to the animal-health industry.

Desert Veterinary Concepts

Dr. Roy Ax, head of the University of Arizona Veterinary Science Department in 1992, became good friends with Herman. Roy's grandfather was a good friend of Herman's back in Rockford, and he recommended that Herman contact Dr. Ax as soon as he got settled in Tucson. Herman arranged an introductory meeting with Dr. Ax at Oro Valley Country Club, and that was the start of a long relationship exploring many opportunities in the veterinary field.

One of those opportunities came out of the University of Arizona's rejection of a unique odor-control technology. Dr. Ax called Herman and asked him if he would be interested in looking at this product produced in Coolidge, Arizona. Following the visit to the plant, Herman told Dr. Ax that the technology would be an excellent ingredient for a cat-litter product.

Having conducted a thorough cat-litter market research, Herman decided to pursue the opportunity. For reasons of confidentiality and legal complications that are part and parcel to this "cat litter opportunity," Herman is not able to divulge the companies involved.

As the negotiations started with the company in Coolidge to license the technology for cat-litter applications, Herman discovered that the owner of the company was in the process of selling his company and its technology to a business in Yuma, Arizona.

Dr. Ax advised Herman of the acquiring company and the key people involved. They had contacted him to make sure the university did not have any claims to the technology. In the course of their conversation, Dr. Ax advised the Yuma people of Herman's interest and the application of technology for a potential cat litter.

The Yuma company contacted Herman, and the first meeting took place at the Yuma Country Club. Herman got the royal treatment from the group, which showcased all of its development and investment activities in Yuma and a wide range of products.

The Yuma company became highly interested in Herman's idea and put him in contact with a chemist: Larry Mohr, who lived in Tempe, Arizona. Larry was working with the company on many projects.

Following many meetings both in Tucson and Yuma, Herman felt very uncomfortable about dealing with the company. His intuition told him not to do business with the Yuma company. As it turned out, Herman was right, as its empire fell and two of the principals went to jail.

Sometimes you should not turn your back on a bad situation, for one can profit from the experience. Herman still believed in the cat-litter project, though. He contacted Larry Mohr to discuss the failure with the Yuma company, and they discussed any salvageable parts of the experience.

Larry and Herman agreed to meet in Casa Grande, Arizona to discuss alternative approaches, using Larry's vast knowledge of chemical compounds to develop an all-natural cat litter. They agreed to a compound/formulation and shook hands on the deal, just like in the old days, and formed a new company: Desert Veterinary Concepts, LLC.

The main ingredient in the cat litter was zeolite, a naturally occurring volcanic material often called Nature's Magnet. Zeolite draws in odors of animal waste and effectively destroys the smell. Larry Mohr has done extensive work with this material. They branded the litter "Desert's Sand Cat Litter."

Herman had mentioned his cat-litter adventure to another industry person, who thought it was such a great idea to the point that he mentioned it to a broker who called on Walmart, Kroger, Target, and other companies.

The broker contacted Herman and Larry, met in Casa Grande to discuss a joint venture, and introduced the products to the industry. The parties agreed to move forward together. Herman had previously contacted a toll manufacturer in Phoenix who showed interest in manufacturing the cat litter.

All the pieces came together - Herman and Larry, broker, and manufacturer – and they launched Desert's Sand to Kroger, Walmart, and numerous other companies. When Herman walked down pet sections of stores to see his and Larry's product of the shelf, he had a "Wow!" reaction. It was a moment of great satisfaction and achievement.

Desert's Sand's success of a premium product became a target for the big cat-litter companies, which use their position with the retailers and their financial resources to their advantage.

Desert Veterinary Concepts introduced a second-generation litter, "Healthy Cat Litter®," with additional features. The company owns the trademark on Healthy Cat Litter, along with other unique dog and cat products like DY-No-Mite®, that aid in healing damaged skin conditions. Other products include Klot-All® for small cuts and scrapes; Go-Spotless® fabric-stain remover; and Odor Loss®, an odor remover.

Herman had a great experience meeting with the Walmart and Kroger buyers of cat litter. The major companies change buyers every six months, so they don't establish continuity with customers. The visit to the Bentonville office of Walmart and the Kroger headquarters in Cincinnati was an eye-opening experience. Neither buyer had any knowledge about cat litter; only the brands that make the most money for them and pay the highest slotting fee, regardless of the quality of the products. The cost of getting products on the shelf with the slotting fee of the major retailers starts at $100,000. It is very tough for a small entrepreneurial company to compete with the large companies, and they know it.

Herman and Larry had a lot of loyal customers who could no longer find the products on the shelf of the major retailers, as Desert Vet did not have the resources of big corporate America. The company is now selling the products via the internet.

Oragen Technologies

Herman had established a great working relationship with Ambico and the Welter family during his AgriLabs years. The Welter family, which owned Ambico, retained certain assets following the sale of their company - including the technology known as Cryptosporidium Parvum.

Mark Welter, chief scientific officer of Ambico, formed a new company called Oragen Technologies, Inc. This is a privately held biotechnology company headquartered in Des Moines, with lab and manufacturing facilities in Ames, Iowa. The company's primary focus is conducting discovery research to provide the health industry with unique animal vaccines and vaccine-delivery systems.

Mark and Herman, Oragen shareholders, have worked diligently to develop the technology, including major field trials and successful challenge studies. That success has enabled Oragen Technologies to launch the product Boviecare® and CryptoPro® into the animal-health market. The product reduces the morbidity and mortality of young calves and increases weight gain of the animals.

As of 2018, Herman is working to license the product to potential international marketers. Herman and his wife, Judy, have enjoyed and are still enjoying their annual Christmases in Hawaii with the Welter family. It is a wonderful setting for their annual Oragen Technologies, Inc. meeting to strategize the future of the company.

Plaque Re-Lease®

Herman had identified the cat and dog dental market at as real growth opportunity. His son, Jay, has been involved in the veterinary dental field for a long time. His company, Shipp's Dental and Specialty Products, has been a leader in the veterinary dental channel. Starting in 2015, Herman invested the time and money to analyze the veterinary dental market, including the products, uses, and efficacies currently offered.

The other driver was an article published by the World Small Animal Veterinary Association that stated: "Dental and oral diseases are by far the most common medical conditions in small-animal medicine." These underlining conditions create significant pain and infection within the oral cavity, as well as the entire body.

Herman identified a real need for a product that is efficient in controlling the formation of plaque in the animals, and preventing the accumulation of tartar.

Someone in an unrelated field contacted Herman and wanted him to meet a person who was representing a company with a new delivery system – namely, a strip technology that dissolves in the oral cavity (both human and animal) to deliver the active ingredients while by-passing gastrointestinal activation.

Herman contacted the "Strip Company," located in California, and started evaluating their technology - including their prior work done in the oral cavities of dogs with a never-used a compound. The compound and its application was strictly based on published research papers, and the company had conducted a small trial with non-conclusive results.

Herman had previously worked on a dental spray with his friend and business associate David Wood - owner of ABS Corporation in Omaha, Nebraska - using a cranberry extract as an active ingredient. Herman had previously shared his strip idea with David, who was very intrigued by this unique delivery system.

David had done a human trial with the cranberry extract in France with great results, and he encouraged Herman to use the cranberry extract in his proposed dental product. They agreed to work with the strip manufacturer to load the strip with the cranberry extract, and to conduct a 10-dog study to confirm the efficacy of the cranberry extract delivered in the oral cavity of dogs and cats. This study directly evaluated and demonstrated the reduction of plaque, tartar, and bad breath compared to a leading brand of dental hygiene chews.

Still, the "strip technology" became too expensive and experienced too many packaging issues; this concerned both David and Herman. David, being a formulation expert, proposed a quick-release tablet to Herman instead of the strip. Herman agreed.

Plaque Re-Lease for dogs and cats is due to be introduced by year-end of 2018.

SenesTech, Inc.

Herman and Judy were visiting friends in Hawaii over the Christmas holidays in 2013, and they all got invited to a Christmas dinner at the home of the former head of Livermore National Laboratory. Herman's friend had informed the Livermore official about his animal-health background, and he was most anxious to tell Herman about a "rat" birth-control product. His niece worked for a company in Flagstaff, Arizona named SenesTech, Inc. This business was developing a fertility-control product to limit the rat population and the economic losses the rats cause.

Herman was very familiar with rat-bait business, as his former associate's company manufactured and marketed rat baits. He arranged to meet the two co-founders of the company, so they could explore different avenues to commercialize the technology. SenesTech also needed additional capital to continue its work for final EPA approval.

Herman brokered a licensing agreement with a major rat-bait manufacturer. The agreement contained numerous milestones that SenesTech had to achieve; Herman's fee for his services depended on it.

Sometimes the intent of the parties in a legal document is contested, even though the parties had a mutual understanding of the issues at the time of execution. By mutual agreement, the licensing agreement that Herman had brokered was cancelled, Herman's potential fees (substantial) went south. SenesTech went public at $8 per share, a price leveraged by the agreement Herman had brokered. As of this writing, the shares are trading at 68 cents.

Despite all the ups and downs of this agreement, the technology has tremendous potential.

Herman believes that no one always wins. Some days, the most successful and resourceful individual will experience defeat. But there is always tomorrow - after you have done your best.

Neogen Corporation

In closing this chapter on Net Vet Supply and consulting, Herman has to mention his long association with his friend Jim Herbert, founder of Neogen Corporation. Jim and Herman met and became friends in Illinois when Jim was the head of DeKalb Ag in DeKalb, and Herman had Wholesale Veterinary Supply in Rockford.

Jim's entrepreneurial spirt and vision led to his establishing Neogen Corporation in Lansing, Michigan. He has built the company with a global presence. Neogen has revenues exceeding $400 million annually, which rewards shareholders immensely; shares recently traded near $100 per share after five splits.

Jim asked Herman to serve on Neogen's Animal Safety Advisory Committee in 2005, following Herman's full-time AgriLabs commitment. Herman has presented numerous development opportunities to the group and provides consulting services. He is still serving on the committee in 2018.

Meanwhile, Herman's ongoing consulting business is challenged by new innovative opportunities, including discoveries by the University of Arizona's "Tech Launch Arizona."

Herman is driven by the great opportunities America provides - for everyone that has faith and trust and believes in miracles.

Chapter **16**

Faith, Churches And Friends

Throughout his life, Herman's Christian faith and the Lutheran church has played a central role. Wherever they have lived, he and his family have centered their social lives around the church. And his faith in God has carried him through his worst times.

Back in Germany during the atheistic Communist days, the government was hostile toward religion. It wasn't illegal to attend church, but people looked down on you if you did. Still, many Catholics and Lutherans – the only two kinds of Christians in Germany at the time – stuck with church and faith, like in the good old days before Communism.

"The churches were the center of people's lives," Herman says.

Herman's parents insisted that he learn the catechism, and attend confirmation classes. He took the classes from a pastor who split his time among three or four different churches in the area.

He and his family relied on their faith for strength and courage when they escaped from East Germany – and later, when Herman and his brother stayed at the Lutheran orphanage as they awaited a move to America. Herman prayed every day, and still does.

"They support people in need," he says about the Lutheran church. "They took care of me for a year. They had a place for me."

Upon immigrating to America, Herman joined his parents' congregation: Zion Lutheran Church, located in Schapville, Illinois. German immigrants founded this small country church and formed its entire population at one point. Herman translated the church's notes from German to English, and participated in the youth group called the Luther League. He was confirmed at the Zion church at age 14.

Later, as an adult, Herman and Judy married at Zion – and their two children were baptized there, even though the family now lived two hours away in Rockville. The Zion church – an Evangelical Lutheran Church in America congregation - just really felt like home, Herman says.

Zion – now called Shepherd of the Hills Lutheran Church - is still thriving more than a century after its founding. The original church was built in 1886; then, in 2006, the building was moved and expanded. Now, there is a full basement and other newer features, at the church, which still has many German immigrants and descendants of immigrants.

"It's quite a historical building, with lots of newness with it," he says. "For a little country church, they're doing extremely well."

When the Haenerts moved to Rockford, they joined St. Mark Lutheran Church, after they built a house in the countryside. Herman and Judy made many lifelong friends at that church. Herman served as chairman of the church council for several years, and Judy sang in the choir and played bells. The Haenert kids played on the church's baseball team. The family got to know St. Mark's pastor, Rev. Wayne Viereck, and his wife, Pat. The couples became good friends – and Herman even talked the Vierecks into moving to Tucson!

In Tucson, the Haenerts joined Resurrection Lutheran Church – which was only meeting in a school gymnasium when they arrived. Now, the church has expanded to add a second location at Saddlebrooke, where the family lives.

Judy got involved in the music program, and Herman thought he would take a break from involvement at first – but, the pastor, Bill Snyder, said it was God's will for Herman to get involved, so he did. Herman was in charge of the church's building fund and stewardship, and he served as president of the church council for five years. At Resurrection, like at the other churches, the Haenerts made many lasting friendships.

Al Jensen is the senior pastor of both Resurrection locations, and the Haenerts are involved with both of them.

"Church has a been a very important part of Judy's and my life," Herman says. "The friendships that we made in the church life are still meaningful friendships today."

.

Chapter 17

The America that Embraced Herman in the '50s vs. The Changes in The America of Today

When Herman arrived in America in 1953, Dwight D. Eisenhower – a leading general in World War II – was America's president.

"That's the first thing that you remember about him," Herman says about Eisenhower, whom he admired. "The biggest reason he was elected president was because of the success he had leading the troops in the war."

As a conservative, Herman loves the hallmark American capitalism, and especially appreciates it after living under the stifling communism of East Germany.

Ironically, capitalism has grown up gradually in Europe since medieval times. "The Communist Manifesto," published in 1848 by Karl Marx and Friedrich Engels, inspired people to use the terms "capitalism," "socialism" and "communism" as descriptions of diverse political concepts.

Herman has found that most people have only a vague understanding of the differences between communism and socialism and, incorrectly, these two terms are often used interchangeably. In the classic view of communism, a communist society was the ultimate goal and destination for humankind. Followers of classic communism realized that it would be impossible to switch to communism directly from a capitalist system they deemed immoral. They believed that society needed time for transition. During that transition called socialism, the representatives of the people would be in charge of the means of production, and guide the society toward communism. Sound familiar?

Communism as a political system never was implemented anywhere because it does not work; look what happened to Russia. China and its Communist party ended up leading the transition to capitalism, although they run the country as a"Communist-Dictatorship".

The Chinese Cultural Revolution did not work. Cuba has failed, and North Korea is basically a socialistic country.

Socialism should be a grave concern for all of American citizens, Herman says. Bernie Sanders calls himself a Democratic Socialist - how scary is that?

"Under capitalism, we have a totally different system of government. It's why people want to come here," he says. "Under communism, property is owned by the state, and there is no free enterprise allowed. Wealth is distributed, education and health care are provided by the state, and prices are controlled by the state."

The idea behind communism is that everyone is equal and the same. This may sound good in theory in some ways, but Herman says the results are bad; communism has failed miserably, and robs individuality. The American way – freedom and capitalism, with private property and freedom of the press – is the best way.

"In our society, the focus is on the individual and his or her own progress in life," Herman says. "It still is up to us right now. We still have that freedom. And that's still the way we operate in our country."

Under communism, success is discouraged and even punished; therefore, people are not driven to excel and achieve. Under American capitalism, you can be as successful as you want.

Over in Germany, the communist mentality has largely dissolved, and the reunited country has adjusted to Western-style capitalism. However, the European economies retain some socialistic components – and Herman is concerned about America adopting them, too.

Here is a simple explanation of **AMERICAN CAPITALISM ....** which may not be the perfect system but it's the best one man has ever come up with. We hear a lot about the other systems, but most of us don't know how ours works compare to theirs. A simple comparison of the different forms of government is below:

In **SOCIALISM,** if you have two cows, the government gives one to your neighbor and lets you keep one.

In **COMMUNISM,** if you have two cows, the government takes both and gives you the milk.

In **FASCISM,** you keep both cows; the government takes the milk and sells it back to you.

In **NEW DEALISM,** the government shoots one cow and pours the milk from the other cow down the drain.

In **NAZISM,** the government takes both cows and shoots YOU.

In **CAPITALISM,** you sell one cow and buy a bull.

Liberal America

Herman longs for the days of his younger years in America, when schools still hosted prayers, and teachers could lead the Pledge of Allegiance with the words "Under God" without constitutional challenges. In the '50s, far more people attended church – but today, Herman says, many people and church leaders have reached spiritual complacency.

Meanwhile, the economy has shifted from the private sector toward the public, with an expanding government.

"Where we are today – it's very, very troublesome," Herman says. "If you look at the latest statistics, what is happening with liberal Democrats – they are trying to bring socialism into society. Free healthcare, free college, free this and that."

Again, the principles sound good in theory: Who wouldn't want free health care? However, Herman says, people from countries with national healthcare systems sometimes come to the United States to have major surgeries; back at home, they are on waiting lists.

Herman strongly disapproves of the presidency of Barack Obama, whom he compares to Soviet father Karl Marx.

"The eight years of Obama … he set our country back many, many years," says Herman, a strong supporter of the Second Amendment.

America's next president, Donald Trump, is a businessman rather than a politician, Herman says; Trump understands business principles. He may be rough around the edges, Herman says, but Trump believes in core American values and the constitution.

"My political philosophy is to be an American – in an America that abides by the laws and by the constitution - and live under the opportunities that are granted to us as American citizens," he says. "If I want to work 24 hours and get no sleep, that's my call. He knows he will be rewarded for that."

A real concern to Herman is that 39 percent of colleges in the United States, according to recent reports, don't have any Republican professors. He compares today's liberal educators to the educators he experienced in East Germany. They are censoring history and indoctrinating children and students to hate the U.S. by focusing only on any negative past. The ignorance pertaining to the U.S. Constitution is a very serious issue.

In 2018, Americans are sharply divided. Could America possibly be headed for another Civil War, more than a century and a half after the first one?

"If we don't wake up, I think we'll have blood on the streets here," Herman says. "It so important that we elect the right people who swear to uphold the Constitution and the rights and freedoms granted thereunder."

Abraham Lincoln said: "America will never be destroyed from the outside. If we falter and lose our freedoms, it will be because we destroyed ourselves."

The Socialist Party Candidate for President of the US, Norman Thomas, said this in a 1944 speech: The American people will never knowingly adopt socialism. But, under the name of "liberalism," they will adopt every fragment of the socialist program, until one day America will be a socialist nation, without knowing how it happened." He went to to say: "I no longer need to run as a Presidential Candidate for the Socialist Party." The Democrat Party has adopted our platform. This was said 73 years ago.......We all need to wake up!!!!!! It's happening

Aside from political shiftings, Herman has observed experienced the major technological and business advances of the past few decades in America.

The Computer

The biggest change in American business in the last 50-plus years has come with the computer. It is the most profound technological development since the steam engine ignited the Industrial Revolution centuries ago – perhaps, even since the Agricultural Revolution.

None of the biggest changes in business in the last 50 years would have been possible – or would have evolved as they did - had it not been for the computer. In 2018, who does not use a computer in their business and personal lives? It was not long ago when the calculator had sent the slide rule into oblivion, word processing had made the typewriter a relic, and the Apple Computer had introduced the personal computer.

Globalization

Almost all cars in 1954 were American–made by the Big Three – General Motors, Ford and Chrysler - plus American Motors. Today, that is but a distant memory. American Motors is long gone, and the Big Three have only a little over half of the American automobile market. Many of the foreign cars are manufactured in the U.S., and many are exported to other countries.

Walmart, McDonald's and KFC, among many other American companies, have a presence in many foreign countries; meanwhile, America's shopping malls are full of foreign products. It is truly a global economy.

Communications

In 1950, about a million overseas phone calls originated in the United States, with very little capacity available. Today, underseas cable and communications satellites provide nearly limitless capacity at a fraction of the cost. With the invention of the smartphone and wireless access, you cannot walk down a city street or supermarket aisle without people talking on their cell phones. Airports are full of folks working on laptop computers, and tablets connected to their companies' computer networks, while waiting for their flights.

Cell Phones/Smart Phones

Who would have ever thought there would be a phone that would fit into your shirt pocket? On January 1, 1971, AT&T became the first company to propose a modern-day mobile-phone system to the FCC. It involved dividing cities into "cells." It was the first company to do so. On April 3, 1973, AT&T demonstrated the first cell-phone prototype.

Then, on September 21, 1983, Motorola produces the first available cell phone – years before cell phones became staples. This first phone weighed 2.5 pounds and sold for $3,995. Motorola then introduced the flip phone in 1989. Then, in 1992, IBM Simon used a stylus and touch screen to introduce the first "smart phone," called the Simon Personal Communicator. It sold for $889 and only worked in the U.S., in 15 states.

Also in 1992, the first text message was sent, typed on a PC, and sent to Vodafone. On June 29, 2007, the first iPhone – said to be five years ahead of its time - sold for $499 for 4GB, and $599.00 for 8GB;

Apple and Steve Jobs created it. Now Galaxy and iPhone have a lot of competition. Today, nearly 251 million wireless devices are in use in the U.S. Herman asks: Where have the pay-phones/booths gone?

Photography/Kodak/Digital Photography

In 1975, Steven Sasson, a young engineer working in the Applied Research Lab at Kodak, tested out a new device for the first time. Sasson cobbled together the device, now known as the first true digital camera, using leftover parts he found in the lab. Sadly, Kodak did not move quickly enough on Sasson's invention; the company opted to focus on its popular film cameras instead of developing these new digital photographic techniques. By the time Kodak realized the potential, it was too late. In 2012, the once-mighty Kodak company filed for Chapter 11 bankruptcy.

The mobile-photography craze goes back to 1997, when inventor Philippe Kahn created the first prototype of the cellphone camera. Cellphone or digital camera photos are excellent, because they capture the moment instantly.

The Internet

The Internet is a communications medium and very much part of the communications revolution.

The Internet is the global system of interconnected computer networks that use the Internet protocol suite (TCP/IP) to link devices worldwide. It is a network of networks that consists of private, public, academic, business and government networks of local and global scope, linked by electronic, wireless and optical networking technologies.

The World Wide Web (the web) development has been central to the Information Age, and it is the primary tool billions of people use to interact on the Internet. Web pages may contain text, images, video and audios.

The terms Internet and World Wide Web are often used without much distinction; however, the two are not the same. The World Wide Web is a global collection of documents and other resources, as opposed to the Internet computer networks.

The Internet is the decisive technology of the Information Age and the explosion of wireless communication; humankind is now almost entirely connected. The use of e-mail is killing the Post Office, Herman observes.

The Financial Revolutions

Many Americans in the early '50s still handled their financial affairs largely in cash. They received their pay in cash and paid their bills in cash. In 1951, a Long Island banker named William Boyle invented the credit card. Credit cards allowed merchants to avoid the expense and risk of maintaining charge accounts; they gave banks handsome profits on unpaid balances.

Today, cash is so yesterday. Credit cards and debit cards run neck and neck, with mobile payments. April 2018 statistics show 364 million open credit-card accounts; seven in 10 Americans have a least one credit card. Although Bitcoin is getting a lot of attention, it is projected that the U.S. dollar will probably still be the world's reserve currency, at least for the next 25 years.

Brick and Mortar

Once upon a time, a brick-and mortar store was the center of the shopping experience. Now, online shopping has become the norm for many people, and with it come new payment choices. Most online orders are placed on a desktop computer, with mobile phones and tablets gaining. In 2017, e-commerce sales as a percentage of total worldwide sales amounted to 10.2 percent. Projections for 2021 are 17.5 percent.

FedEx and UPS

The e-commerce businesses (Amazon, eBay etc.) flourish because of next-day delivery, which has impacted the brick-and-mortar stores immensely.

Management and Labor

In 1954, more than a third (about 15 million) of American workers (mostly blue-collar) belonged to a union; but in the early '50s, there was no public employee union. As of September 2018, 7.2 million (34.4 percent) of public-sector workers belong to a union, and 7.6 million (6.5 percent) of private-sector workers belong to a union.

Inflation

Adjusted for inflation, $1 in 1953 is equal to $9.23 in 2018.

Air Travel

Over 1.1 billion tourists traveled abroad in 2014, compared to 25 million in 1950.

In the 1960s and 1970s, flying was a special experience. Travelers dressed up for the flight. In the last 20 some years, wheeled suitcases have become the standard.

In the 1960s, being a stewardess was a glamorous job. They were hired based on physical appearance rather than for their ability to keep passengers safe and comfortable.

Smoking was common on airplanes until the late 1980s. Cigarettes were sold on board and some larger planes had smoking lounges. As for food, some airlines served chef-prepared dinners on long flights. Today, one can buy snacks, and no meal offerings, on shorter flights.

Since the terrorist attacks of September 11, 2001, gone are the days when you could meet family and friends at the arrival gate, or accompany travelers to the departure gates.

Today we have the Transportation Security Administration (TSA) screening all passengers boarding flights. Access is mostly restricted only to ticketed passengers.

Conclusion

So, throughout his life, Herman Haenert has experienced many things, and lived through major changes in the world – both the good and the bad.

It's been quite a journey. Or, as the Germans might put it: "Alles hat ein Ende; nur die Wurst hat swei" (meaning, "Everything has an end; only a sausage has two.")

Hello Dad,

Thank you for undertaking this project of telling the family story. I'm sure it must be very difficult reliving bad memories, but it will be nice to have a written history.

I think of Grandpa and Grandma Haenert often, especially when I realize how lucky and thankful I am to have been born and be living in the greatest country in the world. Without their foresight, that would not have been possible - nor would the success of my immigrant father; of whom I am very proud. You are a great example of achieving the American Dream and the opportunity this country can provide.

I cannot imagine what was endured with two world wars, the Nazi regime, and then Russian occupation. Knowing what had happened, distrust of your government and your neighbors, and fearing what may happen was no way to live. They were brave to secretly plan and execute their exit, leaving two sons behind, wondering if they would ever see each other again. Although luckier than most to have the ability to leave with a place to go, it must have been very difficult leaving everything behind and starting over in a new land with a new language. Yet, they took the risk for the promise of freedom.

I had the opportunity to visit the farm and small towns of Kahlwinkel and Mertendorf, from where my family originated. The towns are quite similar to the farm area and largely German-American community of Scales Mound, Illinois, where they lived the rest of their lives. As I stood at the home they re-built in Ramin – the home from which they fled, leaving everything and the life they knew behind - an emotion came over me, and somehow I believe I felt their presence.

I am always sad that they had not lived long enough to see the fall of the wall and someday return themselves, but I'm glad I was able to do that for them. I am indeed blessed to have been born in the Land of the Free, not having had to endure their hardships and struggles. I will be forever grateful.

Jay

Dad, thank you for undertaking what I am sure has been an emotional journey capturing the Haenert family story from Communist East Germany to life in America.

As a child I knew my father's family had escaped from Germany but had no idea the sacrifices they made and how lucky we were to be living in America.

Memories of my paternal grandparents come to me in bits and pieces. Upon arrival we would usually enjoy some of Grandma's Rye Bread with butter or the delicious sour cream cookies she made. I can picture my grandpa driving the tractor, feeding the pigs and smoking a cigar. Grandma would be in an apron, cooking a feast, tending to the plentiful vegetable garden or making beautiful afghans or embroidered handkerchiefs.

I recall my father had to translate from German to English in order for me to communicate with my grandparents, especially grandpa. I was aware of my grandma sending packages back to Germany to the relatives they left behind and wondering what would actually make it to them. I clearly remember meeting grandpa's brother, Uncle Konrad when he visited Scales Mound from Germany and how much it meant to have him here.

It was not until I was much older and could see the world from a different perspective that I began to realize the amazing story of my family's heritage.

I am still astonished that when my dad came to America at the age of 14, he could not speak any English and I never recall him having an accent, unlike my Uncles' Carl and Horst.

Although I didn't appreciate it then, I witnessed my dad change careers several times while growing up. Memories of playing on the elevator at Hanley Furniture Store, having to move away from my friends to a much smaller house and a new school, so dad could give it a go on the Chicago Mercantile Exchange, to moving again, to a house that needed lots of work, where the carpet and drapery business flourished. Our whole family participated in cleaning our church as part of the "Sanitary Six", the reward was dinner at Lino's, which made it all worthwhile! Dad's career took off when Wholesale Veterinary Supply was conceived.

In 2002, the Haenert story unfolded to my family, when my husband and I traveled with mom and dad and our young sons, Dillon and Ben to Germany. We found dad's initials etched in the bell tower at the Lutheran boys' home in Berlin where he and Uncle Horst lived before coming to America. We stood at the family homestead where Grandma had buried a coffee mug and other memorabilia to hide them from the Russian Army and dad showed us the escape route on the train in the distance. History came alive as we toured Check Point Charlie, saw where the Nuremberg trials took place, stood in the stadium of the 1936 Olympics where dad would go watch soccer being played. After touring a museum, Dillon, at age 9 uttered the profound statement, "Not all Germans were Nazi's". In Austria, we saw the famous Eagles Nest, where Ben proudly counted to ten in German donning his Bavarian hat. We met several family members, neighbors and friends interspersed with lots of wonderful food and adventures.

I was blessed to witness a true example of a generation that had gone through the unimaginable, had the courage to survive and was actually living the American dream. My family's experiences taught me to take risks, work hard and persevere no matter the challenges that lie ahead.

Heidi

Father Erich Haenert's Grade School photo

Erich Paul Haenert, Pa – carved his initials above the
barn door (EP) in 1920 – still visible (2018)

Pa, Ma, Carl – Mauston, Wisconsin

...he: Anton Kerpen, Ernst Jaß, Mehling, Karl Fu...

Father Erich Haenert started Fire Department in Ramin 1930s

cup - buried – hid from Russians

Brother Horst

Horst, Herman – Berlin 1953

Herman and Otto – Ruthenberg 1953

Former Residence, Herman & Horst – Berlin 1952-53

Horst & Herman leaving Germany – Sept, 1953

Airplane leaving Tempelhof Airport – Berlin, Sept. 1953

Brother Carl

Herman & Judy Wedding 8-23-1959

Mom & Dad (Pa, Ma)

Pa, Ma, Horst, Herman, Carl

Heidi's Baptism

Haenert Family

Wes Remington, Herman, John Payne, Wholesale Vet beginning

Berlin Tegel Airport 1990 – Hanjo &
Troudchen after the wall came down

Herman knocking down the Berlin Wall

Checkpoint Charlie, Berlin – Herman-Grandson, Dillon and Ben

The Price of Freedom

Potsdam 1990 – typical neglected buildings in East Germany

Brandenburg Gate – United Germany

Haenerts: Heinz, Herman, Hans

Armin Kunze, Herman's Mother's Home
Place "Kunze" – Back to 1820

Haenert farmstead dating back to 1700s – Kahlwinkel, Germany

Herman's Church Ramin, Germany building – 740 years old – 2018

Jay, Herman, Judy-Ramin – in front of Herman's House, Birthplace

Herman, Judy, Dave, Heidi, Ben & Dillon visit Ramin

Herman and Judy's 50th Wedding Anniversary Family Cruise

Herman visited Dr. "Eddie Haughey", Lord Ballyedmond.
A man and his Castle, Newry, Ireland

Herman & John Goodman enjoying a good time

Herman's cat litter (Deserts Sand) in Wal-Mart Stores

Haenert Reunion May 2018

Herman's first home in America, The Haenert
Farm, Scales Mound, Illinois

Printed in the United States
By Bookmasters